MOM'S
*** BIG ***
ACTIVITY BOOK
FOR BUILDING LITTLE CHARACTERS

MOM'S
❋❋❋ BIG ❋❋❋
ACTIVITY BOOK
FOR BUILDING LITTLE CHARACTERS

REBECCA BERTOLINI

VICTOR BOOKS®
A DIVISION OF SCRIPTURE PRESS PUBLICATIONS INC.
USA CANADA ENGLAND

to
my dear friend Bridget Ferrat
and
her wonderful family
for
sharing themselves
with me

Scripture quotations in this book are from the *Holy Bible, New International Version,* © 1973, 1978, 1984, International Bible Society. Used by permission of Zondervan Bible Publishers. Quotations marked TLB are taken from *The Living Bible,* © 1971, Tyndale House Publishers, Wheaton, IL 60189. Used by permission.

Copyediting: Afton Rorvik
Cover Design: Mardelle Ayres
Cover Photo/Illustrations: Barbara Collins
Interior Illustrations: Liita Forsyth; Marilee Harrold-Pilz; Becky Radtke; Susan Snopko; Bron Smith; Toni Teevin

Library of Congress Cataloging-in-Publication Data

Bertolini, Rebecca.
    Mom's big activity book for building little characters / by Rebecca Bertolini.
        p.   cm.
    Includes index.
    ISBN 0-89693-980-4
    1. Child development—Problems, exercises, etc. 2. Creative activities and seat work. 3. Child rearing—Religious aspects—Christianity.   I. Title.
HQ767.9.B48   1992
6459'.68—dc20   91-43813
                                                                    CIP

1 2 3 4 5 6 7 8 9 10 Printing/Year 96 95 94 93 92

TABLE OF CONTENTS

ACKNOWLEDGEMENTS

*A special thanks to Stephanie Jones
and Sheri Mielke
for their help at the inception of this
project.*

*And a heart full of gratitude to my mother,
Marjorie Stewart,
for her assistance in every facet of the
book.*

INTRODUCTION

Have you ever wanted to spend quality time with your preschooler, but didn't know what to do? Have you ever tried to teach him something new, but couldn't keep his attention long enough to accomplish anything worthwhile? This manual will present you with a catalog of ideas, each one designed to introduce a new skill or fact in a fresh and captivating way. With a minimum of preparation, you can work together on games and projects with a purpose. Within these pages you will find simple ways to encourage creativity, enhance relationships, build character, and uncover the unknown.

Five activities per week center around monthly themes. The following areas are highlighted: pre-reading, pre-math, word concepts, a unit presenting an area of God's world, and a character quality.

The book is laid out in such a way that you may implement the suggestions as your own schedule and pace permit. The only resources required are those which an ordinary household would have readily available.

Within each week you will find quiet lessons intermingled with more energetic exercises. This variety allows you to perfectly match an activity with the moment on hand.

If you are in a multiple child setting, the activities are easily adapted by increasing the materials according to the number of children, encouraging them to take turns, and giving each youngster a good dose of individual attention and loving care.

The most important ingredient, however, is wholehearted enthusiasm on the part of you, the parent. How can a child help but be caught up in the dramatics of a Bible story if the parent is narrating it with excitement and zest? What child could resist learning about animals when his dad or mom is crawling around on all fours growling like a lion? Why wouldn't a child want to work with his parent at catching a rainbow in a glass or making a tower out of canned goods? As you involve yourself in these activities, so will the child. Nothing you will ever do will be more challenging or rewarding!

CHARACTER: patience

OUR WORLD: colors and shapes

WORDS: big/small, long/short, bright/dull

A couple of summers ago, I decided it was time I learned to type. No longer would I approach the computer with fear and trepidation. I was ready to fly at the keys with the fervor of a college student the night before a term paper was due. In no time at all, I was sure I'd be producing perfect paragraphs at 75 wpm. After all, how hard could it be to move fingers up and down? I purchased a typing program for my Apple and sat down with a gleam in my eye. After only ten minutes, I was ready to chuck the whole computer—and myself—out the window. All I had attempted to learn was four simple letters,

typed in various sequences. But to program my eyes to see, my mind to think, and my extremities to react at precisely the same moment was like asking my dog to dictate a letter. Not that I was too old for new tricks. It's just that the measure of patience involved in drilling and training would tax my every reserve. The hours and effort this project demanded seemed overwhelming.

I wonder if our children ever experience the same feeling of desperation at the enormity of the information we urge them to grasp. No wonder their attention span seems short. That's all they can handle. No wonder they frequently return to the security of what they already know. There is reassurance in repetition.

As we look at colors and shapes this month your child will be challenged to process more unfamiliar data. He will experiment with colors and how they are made. He will learn the difference between a triangle and a rectangle. But as he examines the quality of patience, he can learn how to master all of these challenges. He can learn that nothing valuable is ever easy to obtain.

Take a quick look at yourself. Do you habitually flit from project to project, or have you learned with patience to take an enterprise from inception to conclusion? My own feeling of elation when I could finally say that I conquered the typing keyboard was one I will never forget. But before I could prevail, I had to patiently persevere.

WEEK ONE

CHARACTER *Story about Patience*

Objective: to introduce a man who gained a great reward for his patience.

Tell the following story from 2 Kings 5 about Naaman the leper. After you enjoy the story together, provide a time for bath play. Can your child dunk his head under the water like Naaman, carefully counting out seven times? Encourage reinforcement through role play.

Naaman, the strong and powerful captain of the Syrian army, paced up and down the highly polished corridor. He was very worried. A few days ago, he had spotted a white patch of skin on his arm. As soon as he saw it, he knew what it meant. He had been struck with a terrible disease called leprosy. Unless he could find a cure, he would lose his toes and fingers and then his arms and

legs. But the doctors he visited just shook their heads in alarm. They could not make him well. There was no cure.

A little servant girl lived in Naaman's house. She believed that God could heal her dear master. One morning she told Naaman's wife about a man of God who lived in Israel. With a glow in her eyes, she assured the important woman that Elisha would know how to make Naaman well.

Naaman heard about the girl's words and left at once for Israel. When he finally pulled up in front of Elisha's house, there was a message waiting for him. He should go to the Jordan River and dip himself into the water seven times. If he would patiently follow these instructions, he would be healed.

But because Naaman was a busy and important man, he became angry at Elisha's words. Why didn't Elisha just pray and wave his hands or something? Naaman didn't have time for this! It would mean a lot of work.

Finally, he decided to do what Elisha suggested. He waded out into the muddy river and dunked his head into the water. He checked his arm. No change. The leprosy was still there. He took a deep breath and went under the water again. Two times . . . three . . . this was getting tiring. He wasn't at all sure that he wanted to do this anymore. Four times . . . five . . . the water was cold and he was soaking wet. Should he stop now? Six times . . . seven . . . as he pushed his head out of the water for the last time, he blinked and stared down at the skin on his arm. It was as smooth and clean as a baby's. He was completely healed!

Do you think Naaman was glad that he had listened to Elisha? Do you think that Naaman learned how important it was to be patient? If he had pulled himself out of the water after six times because it didn't seem to be doing any good, would he have been made well?

Patience helped him to finish doing all that God wanted him to do. Can't you just imagine him joyfully leaping out of the water onto the river bank after he realized the leprosy was completely gone? God had made him as good as new!

OUR WORLD *Making a Rainbow*

Objective: to introduce the idea that rainbows are a distribution of all the colors.

Materials needed: a clear glass of water, white paper, a chair, water colors, a paintbrush, and the sun.

Place a chair in an outside location, free of shadows. (If the sun is not visible, you will want to try this experiment another time.) Set a full glass of water slightly overhanging the edge of the chair. Put the paper on the ground to catch the reflection of the sun through the glass. You will be able to see the essence of a rainbow. Try to pick out all of the colors. Then take the paper inside and show your child how to paint a rainbow that won't disappear with the sun.

WORD CONCEPTS *Night Vision*

Objective: to provide a platform for the discussion of color and the difference between the words *bright* and *dull.*

Materials needed: tempera paints, heavy paper, paint brushes, a black crayon, and a fork.

Have your child paint a colorful design on the paper. After it has dried, color the picture with the crayon until the entire painting has been obliterated. Take the fork, and with the tines down, draw them horizontally across the sheet. Continue to bring them across the paper until the colors underneath are exposed as if you are looking through the slats of a window with blinds. Talk about why colors appear *dull* at dusk but *bright* during the day. Our eyes see black and white best in the dark, but a whole array of hues in the light.

PRE-MATH *Number Association*

Objective: to encourage recognition of like numbers and shapes.

Materials needed: playing cards.

Lay out four cards, three of which have the same number. Ask the child to pick out the one that is different. Repeat using other numbers. Incorporate shapes by placing three clubs and one spade before him. Require him to point to the one that is different. Repeat using different shapes.

PRE-READING *Snack with the Letter P*

Objective: to learn the sound of a letter and to be impressed with how much it is used.

Prepare a snack consisting of items beginning with the letter *P.* Some suggestions are: a plate of pretzels, plenty of popcorn, peaches (with peel), a piece of pie, a pair of pears, a portion of pasta, a pile of peas, or peppered potatoes. Discuss the letter being emphasized as you partake of the provender for your palate. Be positive that the sound of *P* is pinpointed and properly pronounced. And, of course, practice politeness.

WEEK TWO

CHARACTER *Watching a Vegetable Grow*

Objective: to give an example of something that takes time and patience to appreciate.

Materials needed: a vegetable (onion, carrot, beet, or radish), toothpicks, a small container, and water.

Select one vegetable for this experiment. Stick three toothpicks into the top portion of the vegetable. Place it in a container of water, allowing the toothpicks to rest on the rim. Set the container in a sunny window and check for sprouts over a period of days. Think together about waiting and watching. Read James 5:7 about a farmer awaiting the coming harvest. Memorize the first part of the verse that says, "Be patient, then, brothers, until the Lord's coming." Find out the things your child can't wait to have happen. Convey your anticipation of the Lord's return. Whenever you examine the vegetable's growth, repeat the memory verse together.

OUR WORLD *Finger Gelatin*

Objective: to learn basic shapes and to provide another opportunity to practice patience while waiting for the project to set.
Materials needed: two envelopes of gelatin, two cups of fruit juice, ¾ cup of boiling water, a 9″ x 13″ pan, and a knife.

Mix ½ cup of juice and all of the gelatin in a bowl. Add boiling water, stirring until the gelatin dissolves. Stir in the remaining juice and pour in the pan. Refrigerate until firm. Cut into rectangles, circles, squares, and triangles. Eat with your fingers while naming the shapes.

WORD CONCEPTS *Paper People*

Objective: to visually confirm the contrast between long and short.
Materials needed: scissors, crayons, and the activity sheet (p. 17).

Instruct your child to cut on the solid lines between the three figures on the activity sheet. Color as desired. Fold on the dotted lines to make the pictures look *short.* Then fully extend the figures to demonstrate the appearance of *long.* Show your child how to imitate the paper people by squatting to be short and then stretching up as high as he can to be long. Repeat the illustration several times to affirm the study words.

PRE-MATH *Big and Small Numbers*

Objective: to correspond big and small numbers with big and small sizes.
Materials needed: five balloons, five index cards numbered one to five, and cellophane tape.

Blow up the balloons until each one is a slightly different size. Have your child put them in order from the smallest to the biggest. Liberally use the terms *small* and *big*

to confirm their meaning. Next, help him to put the numbered cards in order from the smallest to the biggest and then label the balloons by taping the right number to each surface.

PRE-READING *Letters on a Foggy Mirror*

Objective: to illustrate *dull* and *bright* while practicing the formation of alphabetical letters.

Find a mirror that you can easily steam (possibly running a hot shower in an enclosed bathroom). Use your finger to write some of the letters of the alphabet across the foggy surface. Teach your child to identify the letters you draw and to form some of his own. Show the difference between the surface made *dull* by the formation of tiny water droplets and the same surface made *bright* as the condensation is wiped away.

WEEK THREE

CHARACTER *Tortoise and Hare Play*

Objective: to illustrate the added advantage that patience can bring (in spite of any lack of natural talent).

Briefly narrate the tale of the "Tortoise and the Hare." A turtle and a rabbit decide to run a race. The rabbit is fast, but he gets tired quickly and is easily distracted. He alternately runs and rests. The turtle is slow, but keeps an even and steady pace.

Emphasize the fact that *patience* is the key to the whole race. Because the turtle persists despite difficulty, he gains a victory over the opponent that is expected to win.

Plan out a substantial race course around a room or down a hall. When you call out, "Turtle," your child must get down on all fours and crawl. When you cry, "Rabbit," he can pop up and run as fast as he can. After he gets the hang of this, you can add another dimension by chasing your child along the raceway. Only now when your child is the rabbit, you must be the turtle. When you are the rabbit, he will be the turtle. After the game, review once more why the rabbit was the loser and what it took for the turtle to come out first.

OUR WORLD   *Colored Water*

Objective: to observe how liquid accepts color and how colors affect one another.
Materials needed: clear glasses of water and food coloring.

Drop food coloring into the water a drop at a time and watch the swirls as the color dilutes and scatters around the glass. Let your child mix colors and create new ones. See what secondary colors the primary ones can produce. Experiment and enjoy.

WORD CONCEPTS   *Object Sorting*

Objective: to make the antonyms *big* and *small* an active part of your child's vocabulary and method of comparison.
Materials needed: household items such as shoes, spoons, socks, cups, and books.

Gather more than one of each item, varying the sizes. Place the objects on a table and have your child arrange them according to size. Play this game several ways. First, organize the items into two stacks: one pile for the *big* things, and one pile for the *small* things. Second, ask the child to arrange the objects into pairs, with the biggest things on the right and the smallest on the left. Finally, have him line up all the items on the floor in one giant line, starting with the smallest and ending with the biggest.

PRE-MATH   *Macaroni Necklace*

Objective: to improve counting skills.
Materials needed: yarn or string, macaroni with a threadable hole or a toasted "O" cereal, and a pencil.

Tie a pencil to the end of a length of yarn to keep the threaded items from sliding off. Count each piece of macaroni as you string it on the other end of the line. When your child reaches the highest number he can count, add a couple of new numbers to his repertoire. Then, if you still want to add to the necklace, start counting from one all over again. See if the child remembers the new numbers just introduced. Include the study words *long* and *short* as you discuss his progress. You can also integrate the character quality by suggesting he practice patience to complete the task. Unfasten the pencil and tie the loose ends together to form a necklace to wear or proudly give away.

PRE-READING   *Color by Letter*

Objective: to identify some letters by sight and sound and to define three basic colors.
Materials needed: crayons and activity sheet (p. 19).

Help your child to find the hidden letter by coloring the lettered spaces as indicated. What letter does each color begin with? Can your child name some other words that begin with the hidden letter *Y*?

WEEK FOUR

CHARACTER   *Patience Poem*

Objective: to instill conviction in the heart of your child that patience is worth possessing.

Tell the following story with an emphasis on the poem. Repeat the poem until your child can say it with you. Then sing it to the tune of "The Farmer in the Dell." Throughout the day, whenever he is tempted to become impatient, remind him of the lyrics.

Once there was a caterpillar. His name was

Charlie. He was fat and fluffy and perfectly content to spend all his days gnawing on leaves and basking in the sun. "What a lovely life," he would think to himself. "Not a care in the world. All I need to do is eat and eat and eat."

One day he realized that his freedom was about to end. No more would he feel the fresh dampness of morning on his shoulders, the warmth of the rising sun or the coolness of a breeze fluffing his fur. It was time for him to build a little house. It would be called a *chrysalis*, a tight, hard shell, wrapped around his body so he couldn't move an inch. But even as he worked to prepare this rigid hull and felt it slowing his motions more and more, he started to hum a little tune. And finally when the shell had hardened, you could hear from deep inside the following words:

> *Faithful I will be*
> *while I bide patiently.*
> *I'll work and wait;*
> *God's never late;*
> *God's time is right for me.*

Throughout the difficult months to follow, when the weather blasted all around and his little house quivered on the branch to which it was attached, he would sing that little song over and over. He did not worry. He did not squirm. He did not wish for another day to come. He was happy and complete.

Finally, in early spring, the chrysalis began to jerk and pull. Something was happening inside. As it broke open, a strange, damp figure popped out from the shell. That couldn't be Charlie! As the creature stretched its limbs and wriggled its body, you might have thought it looked a lot like a butterfly. A butterfly! Is that what was happening all that time in the dark, little box? Was Charlie turning into a beautiful butterfly? Dry at last, he fluttered his wings and hovered for a few seconds above the empty hull that had once been his home. Softly you could hear him hum . . . (repeat poem).

CHARACTER *Balancing Books*

Objective: to work on a new skill that takes practice and patience to develop.

Demonstrate the erect posture needed to walk across a room while balancing a book, pillow, or similar object on your head. Let your child attempt to do it by himself. Encourage him not to become easily discouraged. Talk about how a patient person will not give up. Measure how far he can go. Then try to better the distance on the next try. Perfect the method by suggesting he stretch out his arms or shuffle his feet.

OUR WORLD *Finding the Shapes*

Objective: to learn the names and configurations of universal shapes while reviewing the colors he knows.
Materials needed: crayons and the activity sheet (p. 21).

Look for the squares, diamonds, triangles, hearts, stars, circles, rectangles, and ovals in the picture on the activity sheet. After you have studied the appearance of each shape, reinforce by coloring the sheet. For example, ask your child to color the circles red, the squares blue, the hearts green, and so on.

PRE-MATH *Colors in the Closet*

Objective: to enlarge the number of colors that your child can recognize and to suggest that the quantity of color combinations is infinite.

Open your clothes closet and together identify all the colors that you see. Teach the names of some new color variations that your child may not have known before, such as chartreuse, navy, magenta, teal, and violet. Ask your child to place the matching clothes together. How many are pink? How many are yellow? Can you count all the color possibilities? Spend some time numbering and sorting. Talk about how colors make you feel. What would your child want to wear when happy? Would he pick something different if he were in a serious mood?

PRE-READING *Name Collage*

Objective: To assist your child in learning the letters that form his name and to help him find them anywhere.

Materials needed: a magazine, glue, paper, pen, and scissors.

Print out the letters of your child's name on a piece of paper. Look through a magazine together until you spot one of the letters. Cut it out and paste it on the page over the letter it resembles. After all the letters have been found, discuss their various properties. How do they differ in sound and appearance from other letters? Find pictures in the magazine to illustrate and enhance the sheet. Does your child like puppies? Then glue a puppy picture beneath your child's name. Is corn on the cob his favorite food? If a picture of corn can be found, incorporate it into the collage.

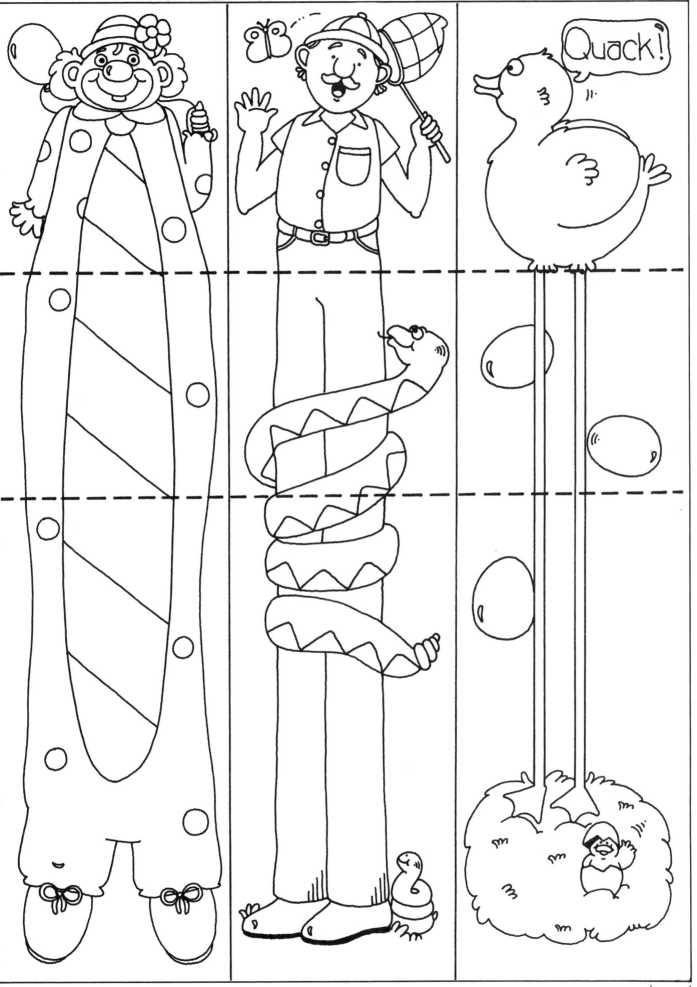

January 1

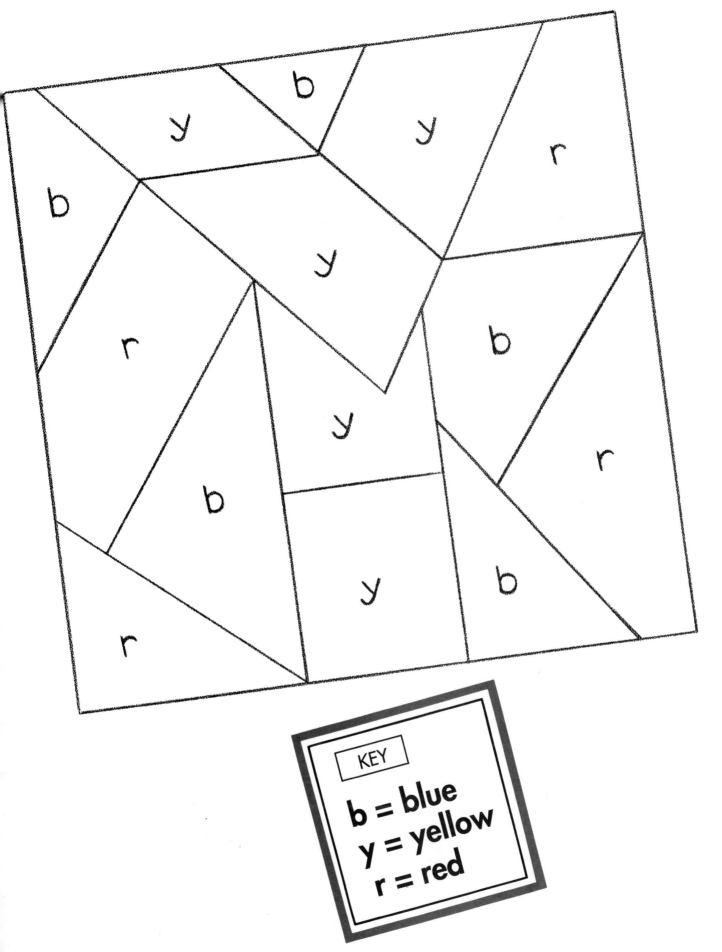

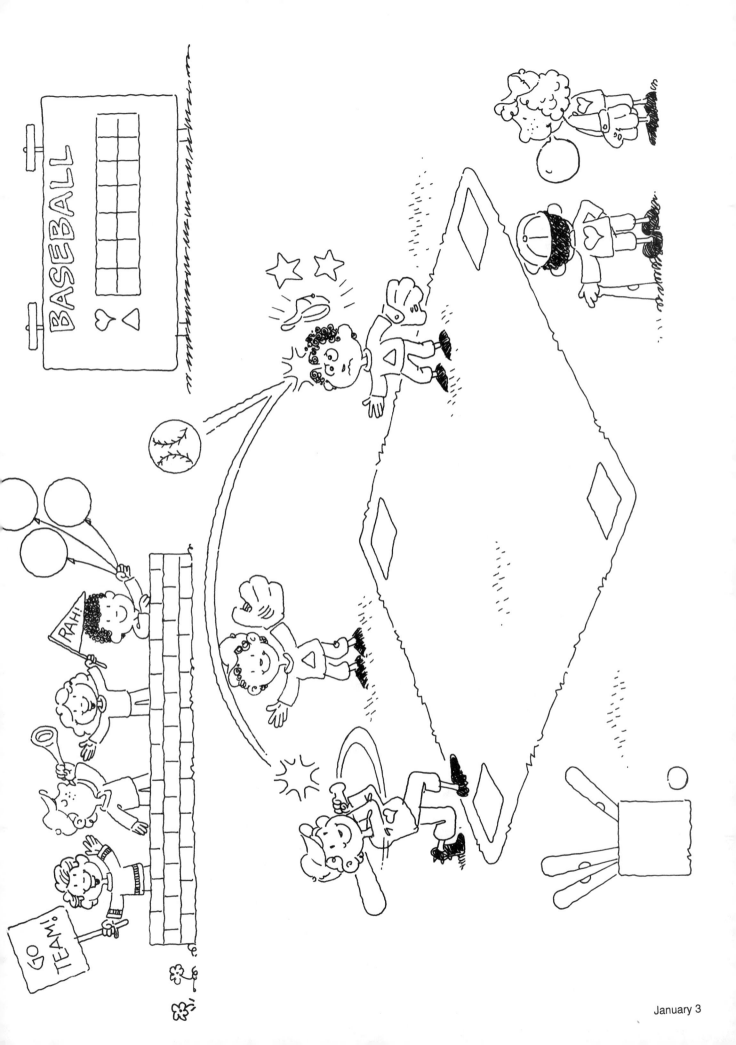

January 3

F E B R U A R Y

CHARACTER: love
OUR WORLD: machines
WORDS: fast/small, loud/quiet, moving/still

My husband shook his head in disbelief as he stood in front of the automated teller machine. The plastic card that he inserted had become jammed and as he attempted to retrieve this valuable source of monetary identity, it jerked itself back into the cavernous workings of the computer behind and disappeared. At 10 o'clock on a Friday evening there was no friendly teller to whom he might explain his predicament. Until the following Monday, he had no way to retrieve either card or money. This cold and mechanized world is the one into which we have ushered our children at birth. How vital that we provide a heavy dose of care and affection so that they have the opportunity to grow up as emotionally balanced individuals.

Loving is not a natural response and showing kindness must be learned. As the example your child will emulate, have you grasped the full significance of what it means to love? Do you experience the sacrifice that true love demands? Are you kind only when there is expectation of return? Do you act in a loving manner when you feel charitable but respond absent-mindedly when your mind is occupied with other things? Do you risk giving your child what he needs out of love, or do you merely dole out whatever he desires? Do you follow up caring words with action? Your child will occasionally internalize your exhortations to "be loving," but he will most consistently mimic what you do. What a motivation!

Our examination of the attribute of love will be a fascinating contrast to our study of the automated and impersonal world of engines. They are very much a part of our everyday lives, but I have yet to hear a machine say the encouraging words, "I love you!"

WEEK ONE

CHARACTER   *The Story of the Good Samaritan*

Objective: to encourage your child to put himself in the place of a story character that had to make some loving decisions.
Materials needed: four spoons, scissors, tape, and the activity page (p. 29).

Tell the following story, from Luke 10, ending with questions designed to put your child in another person's shoes. Which character would he have been like? What would he have done to help? With the assistance of the spoon puppets, have your child retell the Bible story. When playacting, most children tend to deviate from the story line. Some variation is healthy, but when it is time to return to the original story, draw him back with some key questions.

One day, a man was traveling through the mountains. All of a sudden, a band of robbers jumped out from behind a pile of rocks, stole his money, and beat him up until he was so hurt he could only lie by the side of the road and moan.

A while later, a church leader was walking down the road. Would the poor, sick man finally get some help? The church man did not even try to do anything. He just lifted his clothes up around his ankles so they wouldn't get dirty as he stepped around. He didn't want to be bothered with anyone so messed up.

Soon another important man came by. But he was in a real hurry. He shook his head as if to say, "What a pity." But he didn't even give the sick man a second look before he bustled down the road to do his business.

At last a man from another country walked by. It would have been easy for him to say, "I'd really like to help, but I'm from far away and there is really nothing that I can do." But he didn't. When he saw how hurt the poor man was, his heart was filled with love. He decided to do what he could. He put what lotion he had on the wounds and bound them up with strips of cloth. Then he gently laid the man on a donkey and took him to a place where he could rest. At the hotel, he paid a good sum of money to give him the best of care.

Which of the men was most loving? The church leader who didn't want to get his clothes dirty? The important man who was too busy to stop? Or the man from far away who decided he would do what he could?

OUR WORLD   *Household Machines*

Objective: to acquaint your child with the enormous part that machinery plays in our everyday lives.

Saunter around the house and call attention to the various machines in each room that make our homes run smoothly. Some examples might be: a blender, a heater, a radio, a vacuum cleaner, a clock, a fan, etc. Have the child identify these machines by name, state what they do, and then operate those that are within his capacity. He can blow the hair dryer, play a tape, and push and pull the vacuum cleaner. When you encounter a machine that specifically needs parental supervision, talk about it. Discuss how the machine works and the dangers involved in using it alone.

WORD CONCEPTS *Stoplight*

Objective: to differentiate between the study words *moving* and *still* by playing the game "Red Light, Green Light."

Play this simple game together. Stand at opposite ends of a room. One person is the stoplight, the other an imaginary vehicle. The stoplight turns away and calls out, "Green light!" The vehicle tries to travel as fast as he can toward the light. When the stoplight calls, "Red light," and turns to face the vehicle, the imaginary vehicle must stop immediately. If the stoplight catches him unaware while still in motion, he must go back to the start. As soon as the vehicle touches the light, the roles can be switched. When playing with more than two individuals, just add more traffic. Then the game becomes a race to see who can reach the light first without being caught. Use the words *moving* and *still* as frequently as you can to instill their meaning.

PRE-MATH *Percentages*

Objective: to enable the child to calculate and record the results of a survey.
Materials needed: a coin, paper, and a pencil.

Demonstrate how to toss a coin. Observe together which side is the head and which is the tail. Let your child toss the coin a given number of times. Show him how to make marks in columns on the paper to record how many times it registers heads. Record the tails in another column. See which side accumulates the most marks.

PRE-READING *Machines with the Letter C*

Objective: to hear the sound of a letter and to show how machines help many people in their places of work.

Identify for your child the hard sound of the letter *C.* Have him mimic the sound (like a K), until he's got it down. Call out several machines which can be found in a place of employment. If the machine starts with the letter *C*, have your child stand to his feet. Talk about how it would be used and about what jobs it would enhance. If it does not start with the letter *C*, he can guess the machine's function from his seat. Some suggestions for consideration are: *cash registers*, X-ray machines, *curling irons*, windmills, *cameras*, drills, *coffee pots*, sprayers, *computers*, planes, *compressors*, ovens, *clocks*, telephones, *cars*, edgers, and *copiers*.

WEEK TWO

CHARACTER *Finger Play*

Objective: to provide a new handle for a basic thought.

Learn the syncopated verse with its simple motions, then teach it with animation to your child. After some practice, apply the poem by deciding on a project to help someone else. Implement it immediately. Maybe you can send a card, polish a pair of shoes, bake some cookies, or take out the trash.

*Love your neighbor, love your friend,
hard as it may be
showing care for those around you,
Jesus they may see.*

(1) point far away, then near
(2) make a fist and frown
(3) hug somebody
(4) point toward heaven

OUR WORLD *Engine Mime*

Objective: to reaffirm the idea that machines are everywhere and to provide creative interaction between parent and child.

Pretend with your child to be several different types of engines. Call out a particular machine to be mimicked. For example, you could act out a car wash soaping a car, a typewriter typing a letter, a lawn mower cutting a lawn, a conveyor belt moving food at the market, or a garbage truck digesting a load of trash.

WORD CONCEPTS *Noises*

Objective: to assist your child in an evaluation of the differences between *loud* and *quiet*.
Materials needed: crayons, two pieces of blank paper, and the activity sheet (p. 31).

Look at the activity sheet together. What is pictured that makes a lot of noise? Why is it so loud? Are there any things displayed that hardly make any sound at all? Why are they so quiet? Ask your child to draw two more pictures of items not yet mentioned on the extra sheets of paper. Help him to think of one to represent the word concept *quiet* and one to represent *loud*.

PRE-MATH *Telephone Practice*

Objective: to identify certain numbers by sight and to learn the operation of an essential machine.
Materials needed: a telephone.

Encourage your child to learn or review your home phone number. Remind him that the telephone is a machine. As you use the telephone, check in several areas. Make sure that he is following the right sequential order. See that he's pushing the buttons hard enough for the phone to respond. Be sure he can associate the verbal number with the printed number on the phone. If you have access to a neighbor's telephone, it would be fun to have your child call home from next door and be rewarded for his efforts by your response at the other end.

PRE-READING *License Plates*

Objectives: to spot and verbalize letters of the alphabet while observing both still and moving engines used for transportation.

Go on a walk or a drive around your area and look for letters to identify on license plates. Talk about how vital cars have become to most families and why it is important to register them. Have your child state which vehicles are moving and which are still. Ask when a car would move or remain still—at a red or green light?

WEEK THREE

CHARACTER *Learning a Verse*

Objective: to provide a medium for remembering a vital instruction from God.
Materials needed: tape recorder and a blank tape.

Learn the first part of Ephesians 4:32 that says, "Be kind to one another, tenderhearted and forgiving (author's paraphrase)." Record your child's voice on tape as he repeats the words back to you. When he is ready to say it on his own, give him a big introduction. Tell who he is, how old, what he is studying, and how proud you are that he has learned the verse so well. Let him recite. If a sudden case of shyness strikes, say it with him. Your child will probably want to hear the recording over and over, thus providing a natural means of review.

OUR WORLD *Ticking Game*

Objective: to consider the inner workings of an engine by discussing the sounds it makes and to review the meaning of *loud* and *quiet*.
Materials needed: a kitchen timer or a loud ticking clock.

While one person closes his eyes, the other places the timer somewhere in the house. After the timer is hidden, the seeker can open his eyes and try to find the "it" by following the ticking sound. Trade off the roles of hiding and finding. See if your child can figure out the factors that contribute to the noise a machine or engine might make while in operation. Are there any machines that can do their jobs silently?

WORD CONCEPTS *Robots*

Objective: to see and learn the meaning of *fast* and *slow* while observing the value of an unusual type of machine.
Materials needed: a cardboard box, markers, and scissors.

Use your imagination to design together a robot face mask out of the cardboard box. Use scissors to cut the eye holes. While drawing the various features with marking pens, talk about robots and their place in our society. Answer questions about their ability to think and feel like human beings. Mention their function in factories to do things faster and better than people. Discuss how they can only do what people instruct them to do. Then allow your child to put on the mask and follow your orders like a robot would. Show him how to use stiff-jointed motions and respond with the monotone voice of a machine. Ask him to perform some functions *slowly* and others *fast.*

PRE-MATH *Counting Wheels*

Objective: to categorize and count an essential part of many machines.

Look around your house and yard for vehicles with one, two, three, and four wheels. Hunt up wheelbarrows, unicycles, bikes, seed spreaders, scooters, trikes, strollers, vacuums, cars, lawn mowers, etc. Count and categorize the wheeled vehicles. Talk about what a vital role the wheel has in facilitating a variety of different engines.

PRE-READING *Potato Prints*

Objective: to teach the name and figure of an important letter while bringing out the artist in your child's soul.
Materials needed: paper, an ink pad or a shallow container of tempera paint, a potato, a knife, and a marker.

Let your child practice writing the first letter of his last name while you carve the inverted image of that letter onto the smooth inner surface of a potato cut in half. Show your child how to press the potato onto the ink of the pad or dip it lightly into the paint before stamping the letter onto a piece of paper. You can design stationery with borders and headings, make wrapping paper, or create an individualized poster.

WEEK FOUR

CHARACTER *Train Story*

Objective: to cause your child to consider what it means to love others less fortunate than himself.
Materials needed: several egg cartons or shoe boxes and string.

Set up the following props for a story about a train who knew how to love. Make a train by punching a hole in the end of each box. Tie the boxes together with a short length of string from hole to hole. At the front, attach a string long enough to be used as a handle for your child to pull the train. Fill it with cargo (pebbles, sticks, or blocks) and let him pull the train from one destination to another. After relating the tale of "Terry the Train," apply the story by thinking of someone for your child to watch out for.

It is hard for a train to ride down a skinny little track. Ask Terry the train. He says it's almost as hard as ice skating or riding a bicycle. It took Terry a whole year to get really good at it.

"I had to practice and practice," he remembers. "Sometimes I would fall right off the track and it would really hurt. But I had to learn to climb right back on and start over again."

Now Terry is one of the fastest trains on wheels. He carries cattle, lettuce, oil, and oranges. He is the pride and joy of the railroad company. But even more than speeding down a narrow track, Terry enjoys helping out other little trains that are just starting out. He will never forget how hard it was for him at the beginning. Now he watches out for other little trains just tottering along the track for the first time. He kindly and patiently pushes the baby trains along. Not too fast and not too slow. But with lots of love.

One little train kept getting his cowcatcher stuck in the tracks. The streamliners would howl with laughter at him. As soon as he heard the commotion, Terry rushed up to help. Gently he pushed and prodded until at last the little train was free. Then he stood up to the bullies. "This little train needs all the help we can give. You ought to be ashamed of yourselves," Terry declared. The big trains hung their smokestacks in embarrassment and slid down the tracks to their roundhouses.

"It's lots of fun to help others who are not as big as me," Terry claims.

CHARACTER   *Time to be Loving*

Objective: to affirm that there is never a time in which it is appropriate to be unloving.
Materials needed: scissors, a brad, paper plate, glue and the activity sheet (p. 33).

Follow the directions on the sheet and comment about how there is never any time of day in which lovingkindness is not desired. Give a quick overview of some difficult situations that might arise during each time period and what responses would be desired.

WORD CONCEPTS   *Washing Clothes*

Objective: to see how machines simplify our lives in yet another way by making a *"slow"* job go *"fast."*
Materials needed: dirty clothes and a washer and dryer.

Take a dirty piece of clothing, put it in the washing machine and start a cycle. When it is done, toss it in the dryer. At the same time, take another item of laundry, and show your child how to wash it by hand. Scrub it with soap until it is clean, rinse it with fresh water, then hang it somewhere to dry. Compare the length of your involvement with the two items of clothing. Was one process faster than another? Emphasize the advantages of labor-saving devices while liberally using the words of comparison: *fast* vs. *slow.*

PRE-MATH   *Bulldozer Tractor*

Objective: to provide imaginary play related to machines while perfecting counting skills.
Materials needed: cotton balls and a large container.

Scatter cotton balls all around the floor. Let your child pretend he is a bulldozer tractor. His hands can form the scooper to hoist the cotton balls into the container. Think about how much a giant tractor can accomplish compared to a single man with a shovel. A big job for an individual would be a small job for a bulldozer. As he pretends, count how many cotton balls he can shovel in a single scoop. How many cotton balls are there in all? How many seconds does it take to clear the floor? Count the seconds together out loud as he shovels and dumps.

PRE-READING   *Typing*

Objective: to cause your child to see and know letters of the alphabet and to consciously limit his behavior when working with delicate machines.
Materials needed: a typewriter or word processor.

Explain to your child proper behavior when operating an expensive machine. Let him identify the letters as he presses the keys and again as he views them on the paper or screen. Seeing the letters appear immediately on paper or screen is instant gratification.

Hurt man

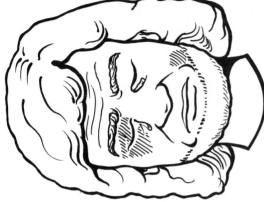

Loving stranger

Church leader

Businessman

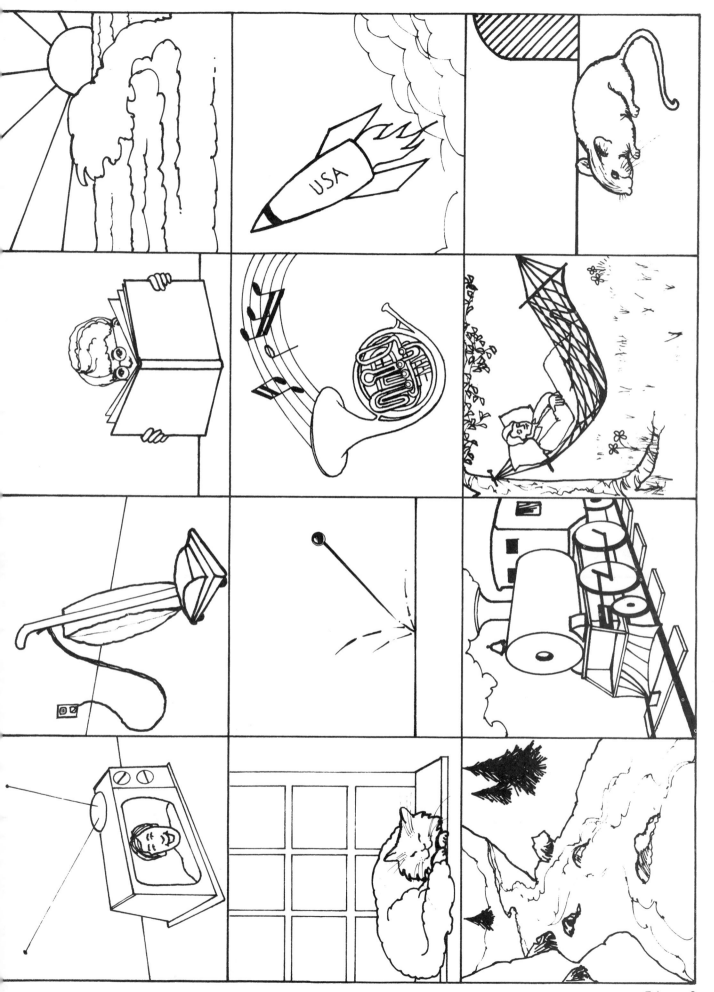

Cut out the circle and the arrow.

Glue the circle on a paper plate.

Attach the arrow to the center with a brad so the arrow spins around.

Cut out.

M A R C H

CHARACTER: joy
OUR WORLD: community helpers
WORDS: empty/full, little/much, sad/happy

Statistics state that 70 percent of all working adults are unhappy in their current employment. In a country where most of its citizens spend their days doing what they do not like, how refreshing to be able to teach your child the basis for true joy. What a privilege for him to learn at such an early age how to separate the dismal and hopeless condition of the world around from his own inner source of joy. What a challenge for you as a parent to check the emotions that vault your own happiness meter from one pole to another. Do you show a constant delight in the discovery of hidden blessings even when they are camouflaged in difficult circumstances?

Against the established backdrop of this month's character quality, we are ready to look at a whole spectrum of vocational opportunities in which true happiness can be put into practice. We will provide an overview of the helpers in our communities. And who knows? Your child's future profession could be decided over an interest sparked within this very chapter. Does he enjoy culinary projects? Perhaps he'll be a chef. Does she appreciate the sound of words as they flow off the tongue? A poet might be a likely profession. Does he work painstakingly at balancing and configuring blocks? Maybe he will become an engineer. At this point, however, the real thrill is exposing him to a plethora of opportunities and encouraging him to experience as many as possible.

WEEK ONE

CHARACTER   *Who Is Happy?*

Objective: to introduce the idea that joy does not depend on what is going on around you.
Materials needed: the activity sheet (p. 43).

Compare the various children in differing situations and circumstances. Imagine what it would be like to be each of the children portrayed. Which child does your son or daughter wish to be? Point out that happiness has nothing to do with what you have, where you live, or what you are going through. Talk about what might make us joyful.

OUR WORLD   *Tools of the Trade*

Objective: to understand that each line of work has one or more tools to make the job easier.
Materials needed: as many of the following as you have available: (1) wrench, (2) spoon, (3) toothbrush, (4) thermometer, (5) book, (6) whistle, (7) hammer, (8) paintbrush, (9) thread, (10) camera, (11) seed, (12) stamp, and a (13) pencil.

Ask the child to identify the profession of the person who might use each object. Here are the answers: (1) plumber or mechanic, (2) cook, (3) dentist, (4) doctor or nurse, (5) librarian or teacher, (6) policeman or referee, (7) carpenter or builder, (8) artist or painter, (9) dressmaker or tailor, (10) photographer, (11) farmer or gardener, (12) mail carrier, and (13) author or secretary. Talk about how the object would make the

community worker's job an easier task to accomplish.

OUR WORLD   *Church Service*

Objective: to observe the lofty call of a servant of the Lord.

Put on a pretend church service. Divide the responsibilities. Include anything that your home church does, like taking the offering, leading the singing, preaching a sermon, or bringing the special music. Set up stuffed animals or dolls to be the congregation. After the service has been dismissed, talk about anybody that you know in full-time Christian service. What are their responsibilities? How can a pastor help us when we are in trouble? Affirm a minister as a viable support to the community.

PRE-MATH   *Learning about Zero*

Objective: to teach an often neglected number and affirm what it means.

Ask your child a myriad of silly questions to which the only answer is "zero." For example, you might ask, "How many toes do you have on your hand?"—or—"How many elephants are in your closet?"—or—"How many hairs does a bald man have on the top of his head?" Teach him the correct response. Show him what the number looks like. Differentiate between the number zero and the letter *O*.

PRE-READING   *Body Letters*

Objective: to review alphabetical order and the general formation of letters.

Limber up your muscles for a run through the letters of the alphabet. State each letter. Use your arms and legs to display what the letter looks like. If your child has trouble visualizing one of them, draw it on a piece of paper for him to see. Let him mimic your demonstration. Have fun twisting and contorting your bodies to represent every angle and curve.

W E E K   T W O

CHARACTER *Wilderness Wanderings*

Objective: to prove that when we are grumpy instead of choosing to be joyful, we often miss out on God's best.

Materials needed: bread with butter and honey and a glass of milk.

Before the story, have your child close his eyes and then lead him on a blind "mystery" tour. Take him on a lengthy walk around the house or neighborhood, mixing him up with turns and switchbacks. Tell him that the trip will end with a nice surprise. Complete the walk in your kitchen with the little snack. Use this as an introduction to the story of the Israelites traveling to Canaan, a land "flowing with milk and honey." Ask your child if it was hard to trust you to lead him in the right direction. Find out if he ever wanted to stop when he didn't know what was coming next. Then tell about the people in the Bible who found themselves in that very situation. (The story is found in Exodus 15–17 and Numbers 14.)

God's special people were called the Children of Israel because they were all the children, and grandchildren, and great grandchildren of a man named Israel. For a long time, a wicked ruler made the children of Israel work very hard in his country. He commanded that they make bricks for him. It was backbreaking work in the hot sun, and he would beat them with whips when they grew tired and did not work fast enough for him.

But God heard their cries, and sent a man named Moses to get them out of that awful country. God wanted to lead them to a beautiful new land that was flowing with wonderful things to eat and drink, like milk and honey. How good God was to them! Even when they had to travel through the desert, He promised always to provide for them. When enemies chased them, God defended them. He even made sweet bread fall from the sky and land right outside their tents. All they had to do was step outside every morning and scoop it up.

But the Children of Israel were a lot like us. Even though they had everything that they needed, they just wanted more. They complained to Moses, "We're tired of sweet bread every day to eat. Yuck! We want some meat. We're tired of traveling. We wish we were back making bricks." They were hot and cross, and they fussed and they whined.

"OK" God finally said after they even complained about the beautiful place where He was taking them. "If you don't want to be joyful with the best I have to give, then you can just wander around the desert for years and years until you finally die. Then I will take your children, not you, into the wonderful land that I promised."

So because the people fussed and complained, and never learned how to be joyful, they never did go into God's beautiful land.

OUR WORLD *Worker Riddles*

Objective: to suggest the jobs of ten workers in your community and to enjoy the harmonious sound of words that rhyme.

Read the following riddles to your child. See if he can supply the missing word. If greatly inspired, work together on creating your own short poems.

A farmer grows the food we eat;
a rancher sells us all our _____. (meat)
When your beater can't mix it, the repair-
man can _____ _____. (fix it)
In case of fire, please don't doubt,
the trusty fireman can put it _____. (out)
A miner works all day with toil;
he digs the coal out of the dirt and _____.
(soil)
Have you heard the doctor tell,
he is there to make you _____. (well)
In a factory assembly line,

they put together a car that's ____. (fine)
You'll feel safe if once you meet,
a policeman patrolling on
the ____. (street)
A teacher shows you how to look,
for information in a ____. (book)
Under your sink the plumber will peek;
he needs to look there for a ____. (leak)
A pilot takes us in the sky;
he drives the plane that makes us ____.
(fly)

WORD CONCEPTS *Concept Collage*

Objective: to encourage the child to think about a whole word category and what would fit into it.

Materials needed: old magazines, scissors, glue, and six pieces of construction paper.

Look through the magazines to find pictures to represent each of the study words for the month. Find pictures that demonstrate amounts, and decide whether they show *little* or *much*. Look for objects that are *empty* and others that are *full*. Finally, see if you can find people that look *happy* and people that look *sad*. Label each of the pieces of construction paper with a different word category, and glue one magazine picture from each group onto the proper piece of paper. Allow your child to take it from there and glue all the rest of the clippings in the places where they belong.

PRE-MATH *Stacking Blocks*

Objective: to affirm addition and counting skills while imagining what it would be like to be an architect or builder.

Materials needed: blocks or stackable objects.

Decide what type of structure to build before you begin. What purpose will it serve? Does the function affect the size of the building or how many doors and windows it should have? Count the number of blocks you use as the structure takes shape. How many blocks to build one wall? How many blocks in all?

PRE-READING *Word Puzzles*

Objective: to take the first steps in being able to spell words.

Materials needed: scissors, the activity sheet (p. 45), and clear contact paper (optional).

If reinforcing with contact paper, cover the activity sheet. Then cut along the dotted lines and shuffle all the sections. Have the child experiment until he forms a complete word and picture. Sound out the individual letters to introduce the notion that letters fit together to form words.

WEEK THREE

CHARACTER *Water Glass*

Objective: to elicit a joyful response in any situation on first impulse.

Materials needed: three glasses of water: one full, one empty, and one half full.

Ask your child to describe each glass. Use the partially filled glass to illustrate perspective. Some will say it is half full, while others will declare it to be half empty. Explain that life situations can be viewed positively and negatively as well. Set up the following scenarios, asking the same question at the end of each. "Which child is full of joy?"

David and Davanna get up in the morning. David says, "Oh no. I have to make my bed." Davanna says, "I'm so glad I have a nice room with my very own bed in it!"

Joseph and Josephine had rain on the day of their picnic. Josephine says, "Now our picnic is ruined." Joseph says, "We'll spread a cloth on the floor and have it indoors."

Christopher and Christina see their friends with brand-new bikes. Christopher says, "I wish we had some just like theirs." Christina says, "I know we can go just as fast on our old scooters!"

CHARACTER *Puppet Play*

Objective: to see how an attitude of joy is far more attractive than an unhappy spirit.
Materials needed: two puppets or stuffed animals.

Make one character take a cheerful role, the other a grumpy one. Set up a couple of different scenes. For example when it is time to go to church, one puppet can be waiting in excited anticipation. The other can whine all the way. When they arrive, one sings loudly and enthusiastically. The other puppet can sit in the corner and refuse to participate. Give your child a chance to use the puppets. Set up a few situations in which he can make them react. Bedtime, family devotions, and grocery shopping can all be opportunities to react with a cooperative or a complaining spirit.

OUR WORLD *Shoe Salesman*

Objective: to observe the vast scope of the retail sales business firsthand.
Materials needed: shoe boxes, shoes, pencil, paper, a money box, and a ruler.

Set up a display of shoes and a few chairs to resemble a shoe store. Allow your child to experience the work of a retail salesman by pretending you are a customer. Let him stock shelves, greet you, ascertain sizes, determine customer preferences, write prices, handle money, and put the items away. Don't look for accuracy, just encourage imaginative play.

PRE-MATH *Making Biscuits*

Objective: to teach counting with measurements, while expressing appreciation for the assistance of a community helper.
Materials needed: a favorite biscuit recipe, utensils, and ingredients.

Read the recipe one step at a time and guide your child through the whole baking process. Especially encourage counting by carefully measuring ingredient amounts.

Package the finished product decoratively and let your child present it to a community worker of his choice, (mail carrier, doctor, librarian, grocery clerk, etc.) to say thank you for services rendered. As your child helps with the cleanup, discuss the roles and duties of the worker he has selected.

PRE-READING *Toothpick Letters*

Objective: to form and recognize letters of the alphabet and to review the difference between *little* and *much*.
Materials needed: toothpicks.

Put a few toothpicks on the table. Ask if the amount is little or much. Scatter the rest on the surface. Ask the same question again. Now, see how many letters can be formed by arranging the wooden picks in various configurations. If you crack them, you can even make semi-rounded shapes good enough for any letter of the alphabet.

WEEK FOUR

CHARACTER *The Lost Sheep*

Objective: to illustrate what brings God true joy.
Materials needed: cotton balls and clothespins.

Tell the following story, found in Luke 15:3-7, ending with the same exuberance that the shepherd must have felt when he found the little lamb that was lost. After the story, make some simple sheep figures by fluffing the cotton balls into head and body shapes. Use the clothespins for legs. As you are working together, explain that when we do things that displease God, we are going our own way, just like the little lamb who wandered off. Share how Jesus, just like a good shepherd, looks for us and calls us to come to Him. Talk about the great joy the Shepherd feels when a sheep is found that

He can bring back to the fold. Let your child respond to what he has heard in prayer.

Have you ever lost something that was very important to you? What did you do until you found it? How did you feel when at last, after much searching, you finally spotted it?

Well, one day, a shepherd lost one of his sheep. Most of the flock was grazing peacefully in a luscious meadow selected with care by the shepherd. But one little lamb, that he loved very dearly, decided to go off on his own. As the sun began to go down, the shepherd guided the animals into the protection of the fold. It was then that he missed the one who had not followed his leading.

Quickly, the shepherd retraced his steps back to the meadow. He called out for the little lamb. It was nowhere to be found. The night grew darker and a storm began. Fighting against the wind, the shepherd pushed on, not giving up. He searched in crevices, over the tops of hills, and through canyons, always calling the name of the sheep. The rain was pouring out of the sky now and it was bitterly cold. But the shepherd did not even think of going back.

Finally, he heard a faint, little, "Ba-a-ah." There was the lamb! His wool had been caught in a prickly bush. Although he had torn his skin trying to release himself from the briars, the animal was held fast. The shepherd gently removed the thorns and put the weary lamb on his shoulders. After the long night of searching, he had found what he was looking for! He called out in a joyful voice as he came back to the fold, "Listen everyone! I found the lamb that was lost!"

OUR WORLD *Community Hats*

Objective: to make something fun to wear that reminds us of the people who serve us every day.
Materials needed: construction paper, cellophane tape, glue, and the instruction sheet (p. 47).

Create a hat (or two) representing differ-

ent community figures. Some designs are suggested on the supplementary page. Are there any functional reasons for the appearance of each hat?

WORD CONCEPTS *Questions and Answers*

Objective: to see advantages in both *empty* and *full*, *happy* and *sad*, *little* and *much*.

Ask the following questions and discuss your child's answers.

If you had just finished raking a whole yard of leaves and someone offered you some ice cold lemonade, would you want the glass to be *empty* or *full?*

If you went out to help bring in the trash cans after the garbage truck had just been by, would you want the cans to be *empty* or *full?*

If you went to a birthday party and your friend was opening the gift you gave him, would you want him to be *happy* or *sad?*

If you were going to move to another town and your grandparents were waving goodbye as you pulled out of the driveway, would you want them to be *happy* or *sad?*

If you were opening a brand new box of crayons, would you want to see *little* or *much* as you cracked open the lid and peeked inside?

If you were in school, would you want your teacher to give you a *little* homework or *much* homework?

PRE-MATH *Hide and Seek*

Objective: to give an opportunity for the rehearsal of counting skills and to remember God's joy in finding us.

Recall briefly the character story of the lost sheep. Then play a traditional game of hide and seek. Have your child begin numbering at a place which will provide a challenge. He can count to a given number while you hide. Make sure there is no skipping or repeating of numbers. The child can try to find you. After your hiding place is discovered, rehearse the difficult parts in counting. Then you may count while he finds a secret place to hide.

PRE-READING *Delivering Mail*

Objective: to learn to match identical letters of the alphabet and to understand the responsibility that goes with an important job.

Materials needed: four shoe boxes, a bag, ten envelopes, scissors, and markers (construction paper and brad optional).

Pretend the boxes are mail boxes. Clearly label each with a short, made-up name. Cut a slit in the top of the boxes for receiving letters. If you desire, attach a red construction paper flag on the side with a brad so that you can indicate if there is any mail to be picked up. Address the envelopes to the same imaginary people. Put a couple of letters in the boxes to be picked up and redistributed. Put the rest in a bag for the young mail carrier to post. With the boxes in different rooms, let the child match the letters in the names on the envelopes with those on the boxes. Repeat with a different combination of letters if desired.

FLY

FLAG

FOX

FROG

March 2

1.

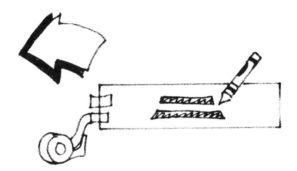

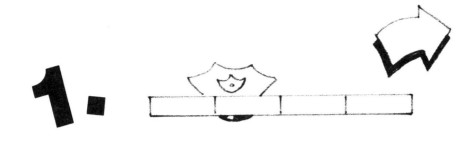

Bus driver

Serviceman

2.

Fire fighter

3.

Chef

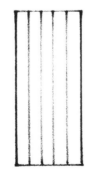
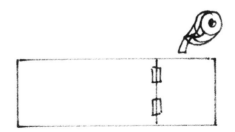

4.

A P R I L

Have you ever met a person who was intellectually brilliant, but had never learned to make commonsense decisions? Or another individual who was intensely practical but didn't have the education or expertise to do anything with it?

This month's activities will challenge your child to excel both in knowledge and wisdom. First, we will explore the depths of outer space. To understand our universe, gravity, the changing moon, the warmth of the sun, the seasons, and why we have night and day will tax your child's mental capacities. But just as important as fostering intellectual

responses to cerebral challenges, is your encouragement in areas of the soul. Has your child learned to ponder questions in his spirit?

The character trait of discernment has not so much to do with knowing what is correct, as knowing why it is correct. Discernment tells us what to do with what we know. In the scientific arena, something like the movement of the earth around the radius of the sun can be logically explained. Discernment, as the practical outworking of knowledge, goes beyond. It looks for the hand of God behind the sun. It searches for the meaning in having one at all. It reminds us of the master plan behind all that is observable, testable, and reproducible.

Might this be a good time to reevaluate your parenting techniques? Do you simply give a list of rules, or do you provide principles that encourage your children to make application? Do you only state facts or do you also promote the exercise of insight by asking "why?" I believe our deepest desire should be to raise a generation capable of intuitive judgment as well as rational thought. That is why the Bible heartily endorses the development of both head and heart knowledge. This chapter will provide the resources to assist your child in giving birth to both.

WEEK ONE

CHARACTER   *Wise and Foolish Man*

Objective: to illustrate that discernment is doing things God's way.
Materials needed: a large metal baking tray or a plastic washtub, cornmeal, newspaper, and sand play toys.

After an animated rendition of the following story, from Matthew 7:24-27, use this sandbox alternative to illustrate the house built on sinking sand. Pour the cornmeal into the large container you have selected. Encourage your child to play with this unusual medium. Could he build an indestructible sand castle? The cornmeal is edible and spills are no problem if newspaper has been placed on the floor underneath.

There were two men. They both decided to build wonderful, new houses for their families. Both had all the materials they would need. Both had the right tools. Both had beautiful spots picked on which to build. But one chose a place sheltered from storms

right on top of a huge rock while the other one decided to build right on the sand next to the shore because of the magnificent view.

The first man began his work right away. It was harder than he had thought to drill the foundation right into solid rock, but he felt it would make the house more firm and solid in the long run. The other man was having a simpler time of it because the sand was smooth and there was no drilling involved.

Finally the houses were finished. They both looked so nice! Everyone that passed nodded their heads in admiration. How proud the men were! As soon as they could move their families and belongings, they began to make the houses their homes. It was a good thing they moved when they did, for the winter rains began to pour down right away.

How the water beat upon the sides of the houses! How the winds howled about the windows! How the hail pelted the roof! But it wasn't until the rising floods began to lap around the foundations that one of the men began to notice some trouble. The man that had built on solid rock had nothing to worry about. His house stood as solid and firm as the rock itself. He could completely relax, knowing that no matter what the weather, his family would remain warm and dry inside.

But the man who had built on the sand was afraid. As the water washed the sand out from under his foundation, it began to weaken, crack, and finally crumble away. He watched in helpless horror as all the walls of the house began to tremble and fall to the ground.

Which man had discernment? The one who built his house on the sand or the one who built on a rock? When we do things God's way, are we like the wise or foolish man? Will the things that we do last for a long time or wash away? Which man should we be like?

OUR WORLD   *Laserium*

Objective: to make a portion of our vast universe a little more attainable.

Materials needed: oatmeal box with lid, scissors, and a flashlight.

Pick out a familiar constellation, such as the Big Dipper. Through the lid of the box, punch holes to form the shape of the constellation you have selected. In the bottom of the box, cut a hole big enough for the handle of the flashlight, but small enough to hold the base of the light inside. Insert the flashlight (handle end first) into the box bottom. Place the lid on the box, hold the handle of the light, then flip the switch to turn it on. Display the constellation on the wall or ceiling of a dark room. Talk about how the same figure is visible in the sky, and has been for thousands of years. What kind of God could create a universe so orderly and spectacular as this?

WORD CONCEPTS *Classifying Toys*

Objective: to learn of the many ways one object can be classified.
Materials needed: an assortment of toys.

Let your child classify the toys in several different ways. First, have him put all the red toys in one pile and the toys of any other color in another pile. Start all over with the same set of toys, this time separating the ones with wheels from the ones without. Continue by differentiating the soft from the hard, the big from the little and the outdoor from the indoor toys.

PRE-MATH *Dot to Dot*

Objective: to follow number sequences and to learn more about discernment.
Materials needed: a pencil and the activity sheet (p. 57).

Review the appearance of numbers one through six. Look at the activity sheet and ask your child if he can tell what the picture is going to be. Point out that he doesn't know because he is depending on his own understanding. Do the dot to dot. Now he can finally see what the picture was all about. Remind your child that the person

who made the activity sheet knew what it was going to be from the very beginning. So it is that the One who made us always knows best. If we follow His rules, we can be discerning and see the big picture too.

PRE-READING *Alphabet Review*

Objective: to affirm the recognition of individual letters and alphabetical order in an enjoyable way.
Materials needed: a ball.

Sit cross-legged on the floor facing one another. The parent can begin reciting the alphabet. Stop after a few letters and roll the ball to your child. He must now call out the next letter, in order, before he returns the ball. Continue, stopping after a few more letters. Your child may have a tendency to run some of the letters together as if they were all one. If so, define and clarify. Repeat the game until your child is ready for a change, so as to gain the mastery over any difficult areas.

WEEK TWO

CHARACTER *Disappearing Cotton*

Objective: to confirm the meaning of discernment and make its application practical.
Materials needed: three cups and one cotton ball.

Place the three cups upside down on a table top. Set the cotton ball under one of them. Swiftly rotate the cups, switching them around until it becomes difficult to discern which is the one with the cotton. Can your child point out the right one? Play this game several times, even allowing the child several turns to try fooling you. Talk about what discernment means. Explain that discernment means seeing things the way they really are. Not only could it help you identify the cup with the cotton ball, but also helps you see things as God does. Discuss the following situations. What would your child do if:

(1) his cousin said it was O.K. to lie sometimes?

(2) a neighbor gave him a magazine with bad pictures?

(3) a stranger told your child to get into his car?

(4) his friend slipped something from the shelf of a store into his own pocket?

(5) Mom said to come home at 4 o'clock, but he was busy with something important?

(6) he were watching a TV show where characters were hurting each other?

WORD CONCEPTS *Follow the Leader*

Objective: to see the contrast between what is the same and what is different.

Instruct your child to imitate your every move. Flap your arms, hop on one foot, stick out your tongue, turn a somersault, etc. Point out when the child's actions are just the same as yours. When he deviates from what you are doing, show him exactly what is different.

OUR WORLD *Sundial*

Objective: to observe and record the movement of the earth in space.
Materials needed: playdough, pencil, white paper, and a marker.

Describe to your child how the earth revolves. As the earth turns, shadows created by the sun move and lengthen. To demonstrate, make a simple sundial by sticking an upright pencil into a piece of playdough. Put this in the middle of the sheet of paper and place in a sunny window. Record hour by hour the movement of the shadow on the paper with the marker.

PRE-MATH *Counting Cans*

Objective: to incorporate numbering and classification techniques.

Hunt through your pantry shelves and have your child count all the canned goods you have in stock. Allow your child to use his own sense of classification to arrange the cans in some sort of order. Discuss the way he categorized them. Was it according to the size of the can, type of product, color of label, or the company that produced it? Which group had the largest number? Which had the smallest?

PRE-READING *Spaghetti Letters*

Objective: to form and identify letters.
Materials needed: spaghetti and a pot of water.

Soften dried spaghetti by immersing it into boiling water until it is pliable enough to form various letters of the alphabet. Be sure you allow the strands to cool before encouraging little hands to touch. See how many letters you can make. If you wish to keep your creations a while, let them dry on a flat surface.

WEEK THREE

CHARACTER *Smarter Than All*

Objective: to prove that a child does not have to be mentally quick to be spiritually discerning.

Prompt your child to imagine what it would be like to be a mentally handicapped seven-year-old. Explain the difficulties that might arise when you cannot keep up with the rapid learning pace of others. Establish a sympathetic bond for "special" people like Elise. Relate the following story.

Hi. My name is Elise. I am seven years old. I want to tell you what happened to me yesterday. I went to school like I usually do. I'm in a special class because I can't think as fast as the other children. So when the bell rang, most of the kids my age went into class 103. I have to go all the way around the building to the other side. I thought I was the last one on the playground, but another kid was still there. He laughed at me and called me a mean name. He picked up some mud and threw it all over my clean clothes. I hate it when the other kids make fun of me because I'm not like them. Mom says I'm special, but the kids make me feel weird.

I was feeling very sad when I went to my class. Not very special at all. First thing, the teacher started to tell us how the earth began billions of years ago. He said there was a big bang and everything came together. There were no animals or people at first, but after many years little things changed into bigger things and finally monkeys changed into men, and here we are. Now even though I'm not very smart about figuring some stuff out, I knew that my teacher was all wrong.

When my daddy reads to us from the Bible at home, we find out all kinds of things. And I remembered about God making the earth. He made it in six days. And we didn't come from monkeys. God made us to look like Himself.

So even though I had mud smeared on my clothes, I raised my hand in class. I said that maybe the teacher had made a mistake. Because I knew for sure that God had created the earth. The teacher didn't say anything. He just looked surprised.

When I went home I told my mom all about what happened at school. She put her arm around my shoulders and said that God had made me smarter than all my teachers. I thought that was pretty funny. I was always worried about not being as smart as the other children. How could I be smarter than even my teachers?

OUR WORLD *Sun and Moon*

Objective: to define the differences between day and night.
Materials needed: yellow construction paper and scissors.

Cut out the figures of the sun and moon from the construction paper. Instruct your child to hold the moon in one hand and the sun in the other. He should wave one or the other in response to questions such as: When do you eat lunch? When do you wear pajamas? When do you see stars? When do you play with your dog? When do you have sweet dreams? When do you open the windows to hear the birds sing?

WORD CONCEPTS *What Happens Next?*

Objective: to encourage the child to think sequentially.
Materials needed: pencil and the activity sheet (p. 59).

Look at the activity sheet together. Let your child narrate the sequence of events as they unfold from one picture to another. Prompt him to imagine what would occur in the missing square. Can he draw what might happen next? If he's really into this exercise, plan and draw a series of your own.

PRE-MATH *Banana Rocket*

Objective: to learn numerical order (frontward and backward) while assembling an edible treat that relates to the space theme.
Materials needed: banana, pineapple ring, plate, and raisins.

Make the launchpad by placing the pineapple ring on a plate. Place half of the banana in the center, cut side down, like a rocket ready to blast off. Sprinkle the raisins (spectators) around the plate and the spaceship is ready. Start the countdown at five or ten depending on the child's ability. (If necessary, have a prior rehearsal.) Launch the rocket into the child's mouth.

PRE-READING *B Collection*

Objective: to hear the sound of a certain letter within a collection of words.

Saunter with your child around the house, for the purpose of assembling a number of articles starting with the letter *B*. Look for books, bandages, beans, buttons, blocks, bonnets, bedspreads, bows, billfolds, and more. How many of these items and others with the same beginning letter can your child spot? Emphasize the sound of *B* within each word.

WEEK FOUR

CHARACTER *Open Heart*

Objective: to stimulate the child to see things like God does.
Materials needed: crayons, scissors, and the activity sheet (p. 61).

Memorize the portion of 1 Samuel 16:7 that says, "Man looks at the outward appearance, but the Lord looks at the heart." Discernment, then, is seeing what God does.

Cut out the heart with the opening doors on the activity sheet. Set up two short scenarios—the first about a neighborhood bully. Tell about how a certain boy would tease all the little kids, rough up the ones his size, and get in trouble with the big guys. But underneath all his nasty meanness (open up the paper heart as if revealing what was inside), he was a sad and lonely boy. At night he would go home to a mom who hit and screamed at him. All he wanted was for someone to love him. Would your child act any differently toward someone like this if he knew how much hurt was inside the boy's heart?

Next tell a different story about a little girl, prissy and polite. She always went to church, sang the Sunday School songs, and put in her offering. But when she got home (open up the paper heart as if revealing what was inside), she took her sister's hair barrettes because she had lost her own. Then she tattled on her brother and pulled the cat's tail when no one was looking.

Ask your child to think about his own

heart. If anyone could open it up, what would they find? Have him draw (inside the paper heart) what he feels is within his own heart and then describe it to you. If he draws good things, assure him how much a heart like that pleases Jesus. If he draws bad things, tell him how to make his heart clean. (Refer to 1 John 1:9.)

OUR WORLD *Spatter Stars*

Objective: to be impressed with the vastness of space.
Materials needed: dark construction paper, white or yellow tempera paint, a paintbrush, and an old toothbrush.

Make a picture depicting the night sky by painting the moon or a couple of stars on the paper with a brush. Then take the toothbrush dipped in a small amount of paint and run a thumb through the bristles aiming the spray toward the paper. The spatter will create a speckled effect like the starry sky. Let your child guess how many heavenly bodies there are. Emphasize that only a God like ours can make so many stars that we cannot count them all.

WORD CONCEPTS *Missing Wardrobe*

Objective: to prompt your child to distinguish the missing elements of a whole.

Dress yourself as if you were planning to go somewhere special, but leave out some of the essentials of your wardrobe. Put on only one shoe, button all the buttons but one, leave one arm out of the sleeve, brush your hair on one side only, etc. Let your child try to point out all the missing pieces of your preparation. Allow him to assist in correcting all the problems.

PRE-MATH *Syllable Clapping*

Objective: to count and determine the number of syllables in various words.
Materials needed: beans, stapler, and two paper plates.

Make a tambourine by stapling a handful of beans between two paper plates. The plates should face each other and be stapled all around the edges. Help your child to pick out the rhythm in one, two, and three syllable words. How many syllables are in your child's name? Call out some words and use the tambourine to beat them out. Have your child state the number of syllables in each.

PRE-READING *Happy Ending*

Objective: to give your child an opportunity to put ideas into words, words into sentences, and sentences into phrases until a story is formed.

Begin a story for your child to finish. Give encouragement to let his imagination soar while verbalizing what comes next. This exercise will enhance his ability to think sequentially as well. The following is one possible beginning: "Once upon a time, there was a plain little star. She was sure no one ever looked at her. She could not twinkle as brightly as the others. Her light seemed faint and weak. She felt so small next to some of the larger planets. But one day. . . . "

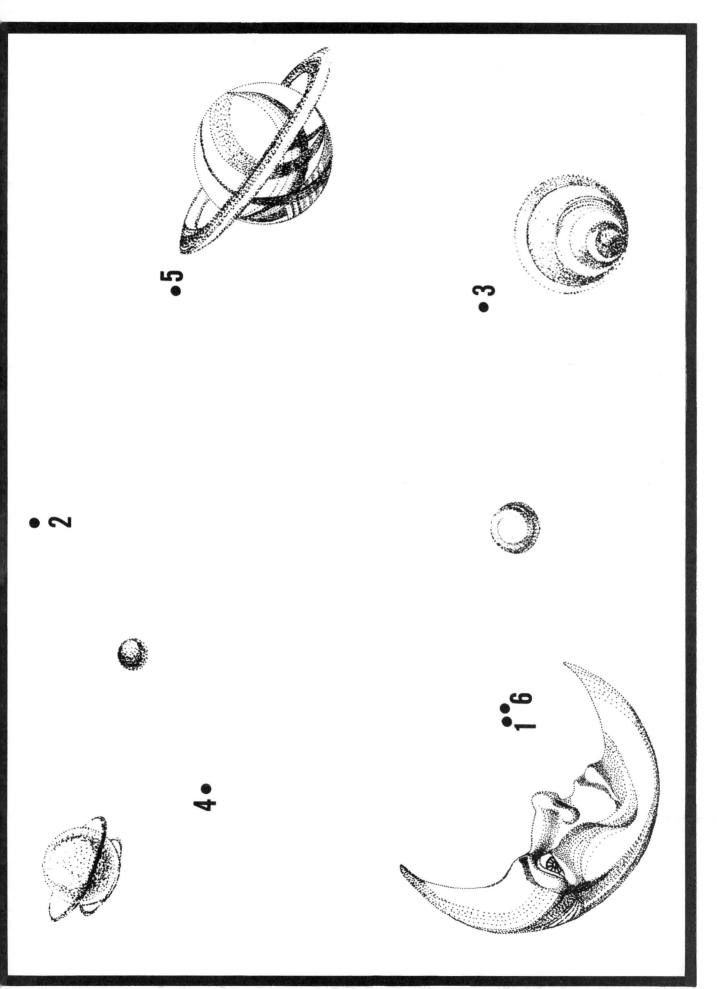

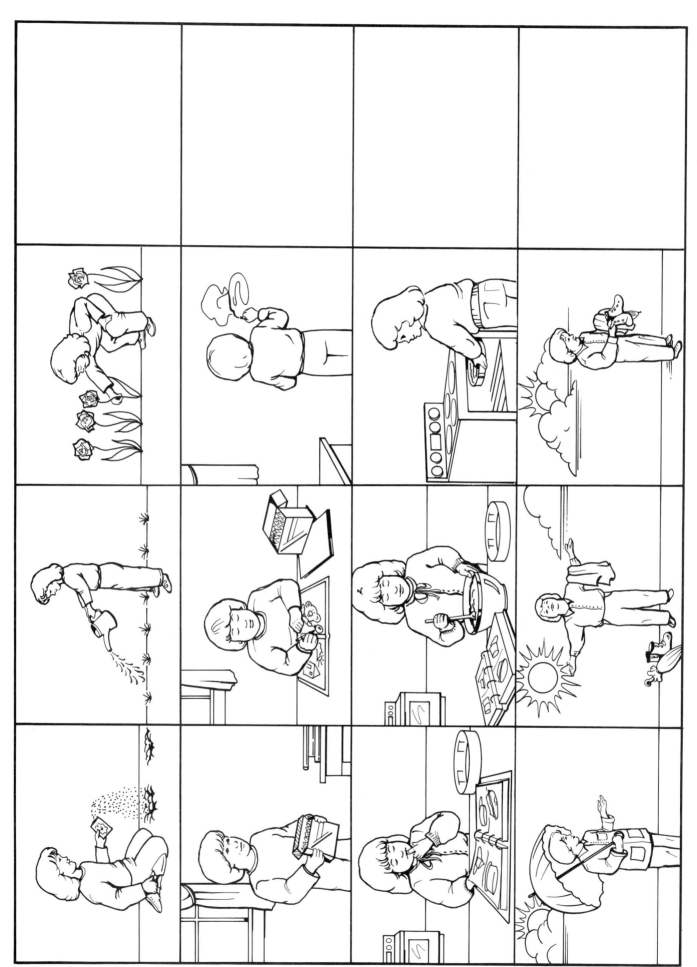

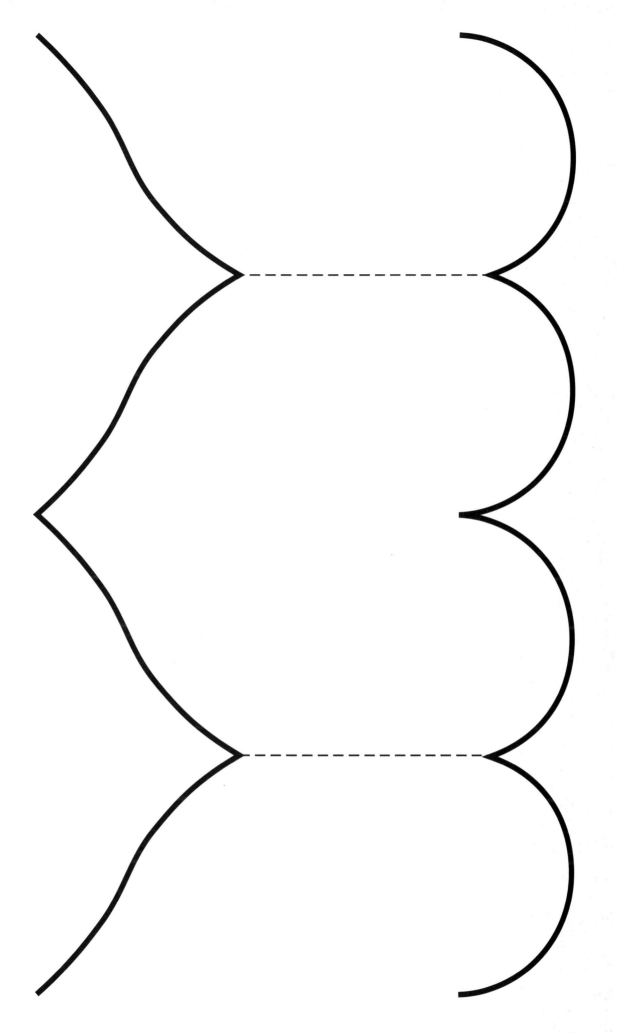

April 3

MAY

| CHARACTER: faith |
| OUR WORLD: plants |
| WORDS: light/dark, wet/dry, alive/not alive |

Imagine Solomon, the richest king that ever reigned, decked out in his most majestic court apparel. Think of the magnificent glory of his luxurious robes and all the dazzling jewels that must have weighed down his opulent crown. Was there ever a greater demonstration of beauty on this earth? The Bible says that even Solomon, in all his sartorial splendor, was not to be compared with the captivating loveliness of a field lily—a bulb that comes up in the wild—cared for by our own Father who desires that we experience the same tenderness. Magnify the compassion He expresses for the flowers a hundred

fold, for He loves us as His own children.

This month provides two objects for discussion that very much go hand in hand. One area of study focuses on the world of plants. What an endless variety, from tumbleweeds to redwood trees! We will observe their various parts and what it takes to make them thrive. At the same time, the character quality to be reviewed is that of faith. Can't you just hear the Lord tenderly assuring us in Matthew chapter six, "If I am attentive to the needs of a mere plant, how much more will I care for you, oh you of little faith!" As parents, our responsibilities can be overwhelming, the burden of child-rearing enormous. Why not take one step of faith in delegating these worries to the only One who is capable of handling them?

WEEK ONE

CHARACTER *Genuine Faith*

Objective: to understand that faith implies personal commitment.

Instruct your child to stiffen his body as straight as a board, while you take your place behind him. See if he can trust you enough to fall back into your open arms without flinching. Use this to illustrate faith. Faith is believing in somebody so much that you trust him with your life. Tell the following story.

There once was a man who was a famous tightrope walker. He would gracefully tiptoe on ropes suspended from tent pole to tent pole in the circus. He would even cross on a wire stretched high in the air between many storied buildings in the city. The people below would gasp and stare up at him in amazement as he performed his fantastic stunts.

One day, he put an advertisement in the paper that stated he would be crossing a very famous waterfall, balancing on a tightrope suspended over the sharp rocks and foaming spray. On the day of the special event, a crowd gathered at the base of the falls. Some of the people had seen him do his acts before. They knew how good he was. They in turn had invited their friends and relatives with excited explanations of what was to take place. As the people strained to see the thin wire stretched over the mighty falls, they shook their heads in wonder. They were going to see a man do something that had never been done before.

Before the man began the walk, he turned to the crowd. "How many of you believe I can really do this stunt?" he asked. All the people who had seen him before raised their hands. They knew how good he was and were sure he could do it again. Even some of the ones who had been brought by friends and relatives raised their hands because they had heard such good reports.

"Now," the man asked, "is there one who raised a hand who would be willing to be carried on my shoulders as I balance on the rope across the water?" All the hands slid quietly down, except for one young boy in the front.

The great tightrope walker sadly shook his head. "This young man," he declared, "is the only person in the whole crowd who truly believes in me. You don't really have faith that I can cross the falls unless you would trust me with your life."

OUR WORLD *Plant Parts*

Objective: to learn the names of the various sections of a living plant.
Materials needed: paper baking cups, glue, construction paper, and scissors.

With your child, cut out stem, leaf, and root shapes from the construction paper. Use the colorful baking cups as flowers. Glue the various parts together on another piece of construction paper for the background. As you assemble the plant, identify and discuss each piece. The roots soak up water from the soil and hold the plant in the ground. The water travels through the stems to the leaves. The leaves make food for the plant as they take in air and sunlight. The flowers give fruit and seeds.

WORD CONCEPTS *Gong Show*

Objective: to discern the difference between that which is alive and that which is not alive.
Materials needed: a group of objects (some alive and some not), and two pan lids.

Demonstrate for your child how to hold a pan lid in each hand and clang them together like cymbals. Hold up the rest of the items you have collected one at a time and let your child indicate those that are not alive by crashing the mock cymbals together in disfavor. Some of the items in the group under consideration might include: a stuffed animal, a house plant, a brick, a pet, a book, an earthworm (freshly dug), a piece of fruit, a tree twig, and an old sock. After the child has had a chance to respond, talk about what it means to be alive. Does the object eat, breathe, or grow?

PRE-MATH *Book Volumes*

Objective: to observe a series of numbers, learning to identify them and put them in order.
Materials needed: a set of books (i.e., encyclopedias, commentaries, etc.).

Review the appearance of as many numbers in succession as your child can handle. Take the set of books and scatter them around the room. Show your child where to find the volume numbers and have him put the books in a long row according to numerical order. Other variations: stacking or shelving the books sequentially.

PRE-READING *Rahab's Story*

Objective: to show how a written story moves down a page and left to right and is made up of a combination of words and phrases that only a reader can unlock.
Materials needed: the provided activity page (p. 71).

Use the key to introduce to your child the words he will need to know for the story. Read the story letting your fingers indicate the movement of your eyes upon the page. Let your child interject the words the pictures represent. Talk about how Rahab's faith saved her life. What made her believe in God? Why might it have been hard for her to trust Him?

CHARACTER *Touch of Faith*

Objective: to show one example of many where faith in God wrought a miracle.

To introduce the story, found in Mark 5:25-34, play a short game of Marco Polo. Your child closes his eyes and tries to find and touch whoever else is in the room. He can receive help by calling out, "Marco!" You must respond to his cry with an audible, "Polo." When you have been tagged, it is your turn to close your eyes and try to find him. After the game, turn your child's attention to the Bible story by introducing a woman who tried to reach out to Jesus. She wanted to touch Him as badly as your child wanted to tag you in the game. But Jesus was in the middle of a crowd, and the woman could not get through.

Once there was a woman who was very sick for twelve long years. She went to doctor after doctor. Each one had a different idea of what she ought to do to get better. She tried every plan. Not one of them worked. Not only did she not get any better, she now began to get a lot worse. Finally, she had spent every penny she owned trying to find a cure.

It was at this low point that someone told her about Jesus. They said that Jesus was the Son of God. They said that He loved people. He could forgive their sins and make their bodies well.

As quickly as she could, she set off to find Him. When she finally saw a crowd of people, she knew Jesus would be somewhere in the middle, teaching, healing, and loving. But how could she ever get His attention? She thought, "If only I could squeeze through from behind and just touch the hem of His clothes, I know I'd be healed!" The people pushed and jostled. But she kept trying. Just a few more inches and she would be there! At last she stretched out her hand as far as she could. The very second her fingers brushed against His robe, she was completely healed. But wait. Jesus was looking around and asking a question. "Who touched Me?" He wanted to know.

Some of the people laughed. "Look at all the people pushing and shoving just to see You, and You want to know who touched You? Why, dozens of people have touched You this morning!"

But the woman knew why Jesus asked that question. Jesus had healed her with that touch. Something out of the ordinary had happened. What would He think of her? Shaking with fear, she crept through the crowd now parted to let her through. She fell down at the feet of Jesus and told Him the truth.

After hearing her story, Jesus spoke kindly and lovingly. "Daughter," He said. "It was your faith that healed you. Go in peace!"

OUR WORLD   *Edible Plants*

Objective: to review the parts of a plant and to show that all sections can be used for food. **Materials needed:** one food item from each of the following groups: (1) carrot, radish, beet, turnip, or potato (2) lettuce, celery, cabbage, rhubarb, or spinach (3) broccoli or cauliflower (4) beans, peas, nuts, rice, or corn (5) tomato, banana, cucumber, cantaloupe, apple, or orange.

Review the food groups by preparing and eating one item from each of the previous sections. They represent: (1) roots (2) stems and leaves (3) flowers (4) seeds and (5) fruit. (We identified the four sections in a previous lesson.) The purpose of the flower is to produce the seeds and fruit. But all sections can be edible. Be sure your child is aware that not every plant is made for food, however. He should always check with a parent before he eats anything he is unsure about.

WORD CONCEPTS   *Locations of Light and Darkness*

Objective: to define those places that are customarily *light* or habitually *dark*, and to visualize the contrast between the two.

Describe several imaginary scenes for you and your child to dramatize . . . creeping through a dripping, bat-infested underground cave; playing in the surf and sand of a beach in Hawaii; riding on a freight train through a mile-long tunnel with the thunderous engine echoing in your ears; crawling across the Sahara desert past dry bones and prickly cactus to reach an oasis to quench your thirst; looking in vain for a black mitten you are sure must be hidden in the back of your closet; wading through a steaming tropical jungle with hissing snakes in the undergrowth and chattering monkeys in the trees; waltzing across a meadow in the moonlight to the sonnet of the crickets and the soft hoot of owls; going on a summer picnic with fried chicken, cold watermelon, and the inevitable ants.

With each scene, decide with your child whether it would be *light* or *dark*. How would the difference affect what you see, how your body feels, who is there, how you act, and how soon you want to leave?

PRE-MATH   *Dozens*

Objective: to learn the meaning of a "dozen." **Materials needed:** beans, pennies, pebbles, paper clips, and a carton of eggs.

Illustrate one dozen by showing an egg carton with eggs. Remove the eggs, and help your child to count one dozen beans, pennies, pebbles, and paper clips by putting one of each in the individual sections of the carton.

PRE-READING   *Tongue Twisters*

Objective: to be able to pick out common sounds and associate them with the proper letter.

Recite some familiar tongue twisters

together, first slow then fast. For example, "She sold seashells at the seashore," and "Peter Piper picked a peck of pickled peppers." Laugh together as the words get garbled when you try to say the phrase correctly. Point out the beginning sounds of the words and associate them with the correct alphabetical letter. Try making up a tongue twister of your own, such as "Duffy dunked the dumpy ducklings' dumbly downing donuts."

WEEK THREE

CHARACTER *Breadsticks*

Objective: to set up a real life situation in which faith is required.
Materials needed: 1 package yeast, 3 cups flour, 3 Tbs. oil, 1 Tb. honey, 1 tsp. salt, 1 partially beaten egg white, and a cookie sheet.

Examine the contents of a packet of yeast. Feel the hard little granules and explain that they are actually alive and will grow when exposed to a warm, moist climate. Talk about how the cook can have faith that the dough will rise just as we can have faith in the promises of God. Hebrews 11:1 says, "What is faith? It is the confident assurance that something we want is going to happen" (TLB). Use the yeast in the following recipe while discussing our confidence in God.

Dissolve yeast in 1⅓ cups warm water. Stir in a cup of flour, the oil, honey, and salt until smooth. Add enough remaining flour to form a soft dough. Cover and let rise in a warm place for 45 minutes. Beat dough for 30 seconds. Turn onto a floured surface and shape 24 ropes 8″ long. Place on a cookie sheet, brush with egg white, and bake in a 400° oven for 15 minutes.

OUR WORLD *The Growth Process*

Objective: to imagine the full cycle of a plant's

life and to realize what it needs for growth.

Turn on happy, springtime music in the background. Act out together the stages of a plant's development. Curl up as tight as a seed. Stick out one foot like a tentative root testing the soil. Unfurl one arm like a seedling pushing up through the dirt. Break your head through the imaginary surface of the ground. Flex your fingers like unfolding leaves. Turn your head to face the sun just as if you were a flower. Let the wind shake imaginary seeds from your hair.

After this exercise, talk about what a plant needs to live and grow. Also discuss any factors that might stunt or kill growth. Let one person repeat the sprouting plant performance again while the other adds essential elements like the shining sun or a heavy rain cloud. Let that person also take the role of bothersome pests like a thorny weed or a hungry bird. Make the plant flourish or shrivel depending on what is affecting its progress.

WORD CONCEPTS *Wet and Dry Maze*

Objective: to familiarize your child with items predominantly wet or dry and to help him think through what made them that way.
Materials needed: a pencil and the activity sheet (p. 73).

Work your way through the maze, stopping at each item with the query, "Is it wet or dry?" Talk about each item before going on. What makes it wet? Why do we think of it as dry? Help your child to move in the proper direction so as to end up a "winner!"

PRE-MATH *Number Tangle Game*

Objective: to insure that your child can identify numbers by sight and sound.
Materials needed: construction paper squares numbered from one to nine (underline the six and nine to distinguish one from the other).

Place the pieces of construction paper on the floor in close proximity to one another but in a disorderly fashion. The game begins as the parent calls out a body part and a number. The child must put the appropriate limb on the construction paper square that bears the right number. This ought to be lots of fun as the player must twist into unusual contortions. (For example, his shoulder might be touching #7, while his nose rests on #6, etc.) Another person can play if you double the paper numbers.

PRE-READING *Sponge Alphabet*

Objective: to aid in the formation of alphabetical letters and to remind the child of the difference between *wet* and *dry*.
Materials needed: a bucket of water and a sponge.

Find a spot of driveway, sidewalk, or patio on which to practice your artistry. Use the sponge dipped in water to draw letters on the dry concrete. Talk about the contrast between *wet* and *dry*. Learn some new letters and confirm the old ones.

W E E K F O U R

CHARACTER *Suitcase of Fears*

Objective: to learn how faith dispels fear.
Materials needed: suitcase, rocks, index cards, and a pen.

Before the teaching session, fill the suitcase with rocks, bricks, books, or other heavy items so that the child cannot lift it from the floor. After this preparation, begin your time together by talking about what makes children afraid. To prompt the discussion, relate an instance from your own childhood when you were frightened. As your child lists things that make him afraid, (the dark, barking dogs, going somewhere without mom, getting stuck, spiders, etc.) write each individual item on an index card and

drop it into the suitcase. After he's exhausted all possibilities, tell him you'd like for him to get rid of all his fears. Ask him to carry the suitcase (full of cards naming each fear) and throw it away. After he tries to lift it, and fails, explain that these fears are too difficult for him to carry alone. He'll never be able to take care of them all by himself. Refer to 1 Peter 5:7, which says that we should throw all our fears on God, for He cares for us. Show your child that with assistance, the suitcase can be lifted and carried. Assure him that God is waiting to carry his burdens as well.

WORD CONCEPTS *The Three Bears*

Objective: to use the six study words of the month within a story, clarifying their meaning and proving their importance.

Read the following story with an emphasis on the use of *wet/dry*, *light/dark*, and *alive/not alive*.

Once upon a time there were three bears. Mama Bear was just flinging the last swish of water from the mop onto the kitchen floor. Since it was too wet to walk on, she suggested the family take a short stroll while the floor dried.

While they were out, a girl named Goldilocks tripped up to the door and knocked. When no one answered, she opened the door and walked right in. But the floor was still wet, and before she knew it, her feet slipped out from under her, and she fell on her back. "This floor is too *wet*," she said. So she peeked into the next room.

"Ah, this floor is nice and *dry*," she said. "it's just right. But it is awfully *dark*." She tried to open the windows to get more light, but the shutters were bolted tight and she couldn't get them loose. As she struggled with the window, all of a sudden it broke from the hinges. The dark room was flooded with sunshine. "Ah," she said. "Now the room is cheerful and *light*. It's just right."

Finally, she could see what was in the room. It was full of plants. But instead of being healthy and green, they looked dead and brown. "These plants are *not alive*," she exclaimed. "I'm going to go outside in the garden and pick a bouquet of flowers that is *alive*."

She brought the blossoms in and placed them in an empty vase. "They're beautiful," she sighed. "I think they're just right." She sat back in a chair to admire them and fell asleep.

Just then the three bears came home. The floor was now dry, but Mama Bear immediately spotted the footprints on her freshly washed floor. "Someone walked on this floor while it was still wet!" she declared in a middle-sized voice.

Papa Bear went ahead into the den. He noticed the broken shutter and the light that was pouring in the window. "This room has always been dark," he shouted in a great big voice. "But someone has broken my window and now the room is full of light!"

Little Bear looked around and saw the vase with the fragrant posies propped in amongst the dried and dead leaves of the plants he had tried to grow indoors. "My plants were not alive," he squeaked in a teeny, tiny voice. "But someone has picked some flowers that are alive from our garden and brought them in the house." He turned around and found Goldilocks asleep in the chair. "And here is the one who did it!" he cried. Just then the little girl woke with a start to see three bears staring curiously at her. She clambered out the open window and ran all the way home, never to be seen again.

OUR WORLD *Nature Walk*

Objective: to use all available powers of observation to learn firsthand about the world of plants.
Materials needed: sack and a magnifying glass (optional).

Go on a hike around the neighborhood, in the park, or through a nearby wilderness. Take the sack to collect leaves, seed pods, or other plant samples to be examined more closely later. (A magnifying glass can enhance the study of detail.) Point out those plants which lose their leaves in winter and those that are evergreen. Look for flowers. Do they smell good? If there are no rules against picking them, choose a few specimens to take home and press between the covers of a book. Look for fruiting plants. Where are their seeds? Can you tell how they are pollinated? Are they attractive to bees? Think about ways that plants are useful to men. Explain the difference between a desirable plant and a weed. Are there any thorns to avoid? Pull up a weed to observe the root structure.

PRE-MATH *Plant Care*

Objective: to practice verbal counting skills, involving an item in the study of Our World.
Materials needed: a pitcher or watering can.

Explain again the various things a plant needs to survive — light, food, air, and water. Emphasize the moisture it needs by having your child water all your house plants. Let him count each plant as he tends to its needs. Ask for the total number of plants cared for at the end. If you prefer, choose some type of vegetation that grows out of doors to supply with water — all the evergreen, all the flowering specimens or whatever.

PRE-READING *Hidden Rs*

Objective: to imprint on the mind of the child the sight and sound of the letter *R*.
Materials needed: crayon and the activity sheet (p. 75).

Help your child look for the formation of the letter *R* as it appears all over the sheet in various forms. Show him how to trace the figures on the paper. Help him to hear the sound of R in railroad.

Rahab's Story

ONCE UPON A 🕐, 👧 LIVED IN THE GREAT 🏙 OF JERICHO. SHE HEARD WITH HER OWN 👂S MANY 📖S ABOUT THE ⛪ OF THE CHILDREN OF ISRAEL. THEIR ⛪ HELPED THEM CROSS 〰️S, FIND 🍽, AND FIGHT 👥. WHEN 👧 MET 2 MEN OF ISRAEL, 👧 HELPED THEM TO 🫣 FROM THEIR 👥 AND ⛪ WAS PLEASED. THE 2 WHO 🫣 TOLD 👧 THAT SHE COULD BE SAVED WHEN THE 🧱 👧 MUST PUT A 🎀 OUT THE 🪟 OF HER 🏠 AND ⛪ WOULD REMEMBER 👧. THE 2 MEN LEFT AND 👧 PUT THE 🎀 OUT THE 🪟 OF HER 🏠 AND WAITED. SOON 👧 COULD 👁 ⛪'S PEOPLE FROM HER 🪟. THEY 🚶🚶 EVERY DAY FOR 7 DAYS. THEIR 👄S AND THEIR 👣 DID NOT MAKE 1 NOISE. ON THE 7TH DAY, THEY OPENED THEIR 👄S, STOMPED THEIR 👣, BLEW THEIR 🎺S, AND BANGED THEIR 🥁S. THE 🧱 BUT THE 🏠 WITH THE 🎀 IN THE 🪟 STILL STOOD. 👧 BELIEVED AND HAD FAITH IN ⛪ SO 👧 WAS SAVED.

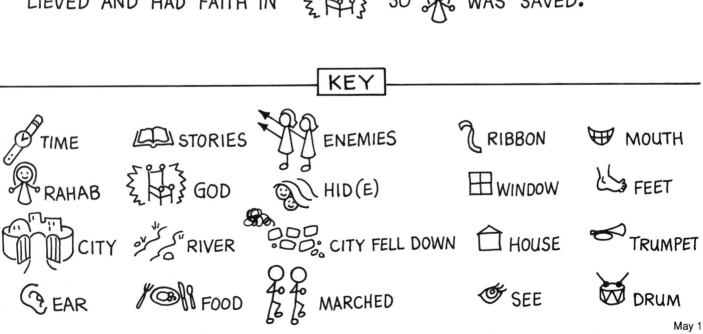

KEY

🕐 TIME	📖 STORIES	👥 ENEMIES
👧 RAHAB	⛪ GOD	🫣 HID(E)
🏙 CITY	〰️ RIVER	🧱 CITY FELL DOWN
👂 EAR	🍽 FOOD	🚶🚶 MARCHED
🎀 RIBBON	🪟 WINDOW	🏠 HOUSE
👄 MOUTH	👣 FEET	🎺 TRUMPET
👁 SEE	🥁 DRUM	

If the item is dry, go up. If the item is wet, go down.

START

YOU WIN

May 2

May 3

J U N E

CHARACTER: responsibility
OUR WORLD: ecology
WORDS: few/many, fragile/unbreakable, sink/float

Americans throw away an average of three and one half pounds of trash per day. That's enough to bury one thousand football fields under a pile of junk three hundred feet high. We toss enough soda cans in a week to circle the earth four times. Five hundred thousand trees are chopped down to process enough newspapers for us to read in one Sunday alone.

Are you concerned about our environment? Are there ways you can work as a family to cut down waste and improve our world? The subject of ecology encompasses everything from recycling cans to rescuing critters. Most important it emphasizes our individual responsibility. And responsibility is the very characteristic we want to look into this month. This includes not just our accountability in the area of our environment, but also the duties we ought to perform and the people we need to serve in the sectors to which we belong—church, community, family, etc.

Have you figured out how to kindle a sense of pride in the heart of your child at the privilege of being trusted to do a job? This perspective transforms a burdensome chore into an esteemed honor. Are you willing to allow a job to be executed at a lower standard of perfection in order to teach your child the pleasure of taking responsibility? When a parent criticizes or reworks every task a child undertakes, there is no incentive to perform. Have you learned to stimulate your child to service through praise? Pleasing you is often his greatest reward.

WEEK ONE

CHARACTER *Keeping the Sheep*

Objective: to introduce a man from the Bible who had a responsibility and carried it through, even in the midst of adversity.
Materials needed: several different sized rubber bands and a shoe box.

Relate the story of David, based on information from 1 Samuel 16:11-23; 17:34-37. Then talk about the jobs and responsibilities that your child must fulfill. He won't have to kill a lion or a bear, but perhaps there are parts of his duties that he considers difficult. What are they? How can he make the job more pleasant? Can he sing while he works, just like David? Make a visual aid to enhance the story. Fashion a harp by stretching the rubber bands around a lidless shoe box. Strum the bands on the open side.

When David was a young boy, his father gave him a difficult job to do. It was David's job to care for the family sheep. This meant he must make sure they had plenty of food and water. He must bring them home at night. He must be sure that not one of them got lost or eaten by a wild animal.

David wanted to do the job well, so day after day he would take the sheep to green valleys with deep pools of water. Because he had no one to talk to or to play with, he brought a harp along to play and help him sing songs.

One day a lion jumped out of the brush and grabbed one of the sheep. David probably wished he could run away, but he knew what his job was, so he wrestled the lion to the ground and killed it. He also became very good with a sling shot and one time killed a bear.

Because David did so well at this difficult job when he was a boy, God gave him a bigger and more important job when he was a man. He became a king!

OUR WORLD *Our Environment*

Objective: to see what man has done to his environment.
Materials needed: crayons and the activity sheet (p. 85).

Take a look at the two scenes for comparison. Have your child add the finishing touches. Instruct him to draw soaring birds, splashing fish, new green saplings, a blue sky, and lush, green grass to complete the picture on the top. To the bottom picture he can add cars and buses, flashy billboards, traffic lights, smoke from factory chimneys, and a flat, grey sky.

Where would he rather live? What are the differences? How did each scene come about? Is it too late to change anything?

WORD CONCEPTS *Fragile Dishes*

Objective: to create an indelible impression of what it means when a parent warns that something is *fragile*.
Materials needed: two pairs of sunglasses or goggles, a breakable (not precious) dish or mug, and an unbreakable (plastic) dish or mug.

Go to a place where you can break an object and easily sweep it up. Stand up and away from any splintering pieces and wear protective coverings for eyes and feet. Bounce the unbreakable dish off the floor. Examine it and the ground for broken pieces and/or messes. Then drop the breakable one. Watch it shatter. Why did one break while the other did not? Talk about the sights and sounds of an object exploding into a million pieces on the ground. As the parent sweeps the floor, show the child the jagged remainders on their way to the trash. Walk around the house and let the child point out what is *fragile* and what is *unbreakable*.

PRE-MATH *Sinkable and Floatable*

Objective: to number and keep accounts while experimenting with how objects respond in water.
Materials needed: a variety of items that will either sink or float and a tub full of water.

Drop each object into the water and watch what happens. Does it *sink* or does it *float?* Keep a running tabulation by dividing a sheet of paper in half and making marks. Count up all the marks at the end. Learn through experimentation.

PRE-READING *Name Rub*

Objective: to work on the recognition and formation of the letters within the child's name.
Materials needed: piece of cardboard, pencil, glue, paper, and crayons.

In pencil, have the child write as many letters in his name as he can. Work on the remaining letters until his name is sketched in bold letters on the cardboard. Follow the contours of the letters with paper glue, making nice thick lines. Let it fully dry. Lay a piece of white paper over the design. Rub a crayon sideways over the bumpy letters to create an impression of the child's name.

W E E K   T W O

CHARACTER *To the Glory of God*

Objective: to affirm that whatever the job, our motivation should be the Lord's approval.

Learn 1 Corinthians 10:31 with a few simple motions:

"Whether you eat
(Bring imaginary fork to your mouth.)
or drink
(Lift pretend cup to your lips.)
or whatever you do
(Spread hands wide with a shrug.)
do it all for the glory of God."
(Point heavenward.)

After your child has the verse down, ask some rhetorical questions to reinforce the point:

Q. How should I eat?
A. to the glory of God
Q. How should I play?
A. to the glory of God
Q. How should I do chores?
A. to the glory of God

Continue with more questions along these lines, allowing your child to supply the answers.

OUR WORLD *Trash Bag*

Objective: to make a practical aid in the cleaning up of our environment and to let the child take some responsibility in this area.
Materials needed: a lunch-sized paper bag, paints, brushes, and scissors.

Let your child colorfully decorate the bag with paint. After it dries, cut a small hole near the top. The bag can be placed over a switch or knob on the dash of your car as a trash catcher. Let your child present it as a gift to the family and explain its use. When traveling, remind your child of its presence and when to make use of it. Let it be his responsibility to empty the bag after each trip and put it back in its place.

WORD CONCEPTS *Sail Boat*

Objective: to understand why boats stay on top of the water in a further study of *sink* and *float*.
Materials needed: a small plastic bowl, play-

dough, a short stick (popsicle, if available), cellophane tape, and a small square of paper.

Make a sailing vessel with your own embellishments but following this basic design. Put a dab of playdough in the center of the bowl to hold the stick upright. Tape the paper to the top of the stick to serve as a sail. Try out your boat in water. Does it *float?* Why? Explain that air is lighter than water. The bottom of the boat holds out the water. That is how a heavy ship can stay on top of the sea.

PRE-MATH *Sandbox Numbers*

Objective: to practice the writing of numbers in a different medium.

Find some sand at a park or in your own backyard. Dampen it with water enough to allow it to hold some shape. With a stick or spoon, work together on sketching some numbers in the sand. Begin with numbers the child knows and continue by adding others that are unfamiliar. Incorporate the concept of *few/many* by asking the child to estimate the number of grains of sand.

PRE-READING *Picture Definitions*

Objective: to help the child hear the sound of *H* at the beginning of some common words and to add to the child's vocabulary.
Materials needed: old magazines, scissors, glue, construction paper, and a thin marker.

At the top of the first construction paper page, help the child to write an *H.* Then thumb through the magazines looking for pictures of words that start with *H.* Let your child cut them out and glue them on the page you have begun. Add extra sheets as needed. After you have quite a few pictures, go back to each one and let the child state the item and make up his own definition of what it is. (For example, hat = something you wear on your head.) Write next to the corresponding picture your child's words as he dictates. The definitions can be quite hi-

larious. It will provide fun reading for years ahead as well as being a current indicator of the child's comprehension of the English language.

WEEK THREE

CHARACTER *Prayer Duties*

Objective: to show that we have a Christian responsibility to uphold others in the area of prayer.
Materials needed: index cards, photos of people to pray for, glue, and a marker.

After telling the following short story about a little girl and her prayer life, compare her struggles with that of your child's. Take the index cards and glue a photo on each with the names of those people the child would like to remember in prayer. Use these cards during prayer time as visual prompters of specific individuals and their needs. Discuss what areas to cover in prayer for each person. Divide the cards into days of the week or use them all every day.

"Dear God," prayed Laurie. "Thank you for the food. Amen." She looked up smiling. Oh no! She had made a big mistake. There was no plate in front of her. It was night time and she was kneeling beside her bed.

"Better try again," said her mommy gently. "But this time remember what you are doing. You're talking to God about your day."

Laurie started once more. "Dear God, bless Mommy and Daddy and Grandma and Grandpa and the kitty . . ." her voice trailed off. She started thinking about how roly-poly and cuddly-soft her kitty was.

"Honey, let's talk for a minute," said her mother, getting down on her knees beside her. "Suppose we were talking together on the phone. What if I decided to do something else and just dropped the receiver and left you hanging there? Or suppose every time I talked to you, I said the same things over and over? Or suppose I didn't make any sense at all, I just babbled on and on. You would think I didn't care much about you, wouldn't you? When you talk to God, it's just the same. Don't leave Him hanging, or say the same things over and over as if they have no meaning. Talk to Him like you would talk to me. You can't see Him, but He's there, just like I would still be on the phone even if you could not see me. We should take the same care in talking to God that we would in speaking with anyone else we love."

Laurie smiled, "I'll try, Mom!"

OUR WORLD   *Recycling*

Objective: to train the child to use items normally discarded in practical ways.
Materials needed: an empty can, glue, paper, and markers.

Make a pencil holder out of an empty soup or vegetable can by covering it with paper and drawing beautiful designs on the outside. Talk about the enormous volume of trash that each family discards every day. Take a look at the containers your own family fills each week with refuse. Think of other ways to use throwaways more than once. Check into paper, aluminum can, glass, and plastic recycling and put a plan into action for your own family.

WORD CONCEPTS   *Counting Coins*

Objective: to give the opportunity to consider *few* and *many* while learning how to add.
Materials needed: a handful of coins.

Ask if there are many coins or few. Count them. Divide into denominations: how many pennies, nickels, dimes and quarters? Are there many in any particular category? Are there only a few of another? Put two types of coins together. Does it seem like many more? Count them. What about shiny, new ones? *Few* or *many?*

PRE-MATH   *Picking Up Trash*

Objective: to encourage counting, particularly of numbers over twenty, while reinforcing the topic of ecology.
Materials needed: a trash bag, gloves and/or small plastic bags.

Take a trash bag and find a street or park where people have carelessly strewn their litter and garbage. Put gloves or baggies on your hands to keep them clean. Count each piece of trash as you put it in your bag. Talk about what the world would be like if everyone threw anything they no longer wanted on the ground. What should be done with the trash instead? Where does the trash go from there?

PRE-READING   *Eggshell Letter*

Objective: to learn the formation of another letter with its accompanying sound and to discuss *fragile/unbreakable* in a different forum.
Materials needed: glue, eggshells (broken and washed), and brightly colored construction paper.

Draw the outline of an alphabetical letter onto the construction paper. Let the child apply glue within the boundaries of the letter. What sound does the letter make? Think of words that involve that letter. Place the broken shells into the glue to form an eggshell letter. Talk about eggs. Are they *fragile* or *unbreakable?* Why would God make an eggshell so delicate?

WEEK FOUR

CHARACTER   *Jonah's Responsibility*

Objective: to look at a man who ran away from responsibility.
Materials needed: crayons, scissors and the

activity sheet (p. 87).

Tell the story of Jonah, found in the book of the Bible with the same name, using the paperwork activity to reinforce what was learned. What happens when people do not fulfill their responsibilities? Review the responsibilities of your child. He won't be swallowed by a big fish if he doesn't do his chores, but what would happen if they were neglected? Would God be pleased? Use the figures to tell the story again.

God had given Jonah a very important job. There was a city where everybody who lived within its walls was evil. Not one person pleased God! God told Jonah to go to the city and tell the people how unhappy He was that they did bad things. If they did not change, God would completely wipe out the city.

Jonah did not want to do the job God had given him. So he decided to get out of it by running away and hiding from God. He took a boat heading in the opposite direction and went down to the very bottom of that boat, hoping that God would not notice him there.

But God knew exactly where Jonah was and sent a big storm. Everyone on the boat was afraid. Finally, Jonah came up and told them he guessed he had caused the storm by running away from God. So the people on the boat threw him over the side.

But God did not let him drown. He sent a big fish to swallow him. You can imagine how awful it was to live in the tummy of a fish! Finally, the fish swam to dry land and threw him up on the shore.

By this time, Jonah asked God's forgiveness and started off to do the job God had told him to do at the beginning. He realized that when someone gives you a responsibility, it isn't wise to try to get out of it. Not only does the job still need to be done, but the person doing the job misses out on a lot as well.

When Jonah got to the city and called out God's warnings, everyone in the city turned from evil to worship God.

OUR WORLD *What's Wrong?*

Objective: to prompt the child to think of ways to conserve energy and save the environment by isolating and rectifying negative examples.

Before you begin, do the following within your house: (1) turn on all sources of water and leave them running; (2) turn on lights, television, and various other electrical appliances that can be left on; (3) strew paper trash around the floor; and (4) turn on the thermostat to use heat or air.

Ask your child to notice and rectify any poor examples of ecology in action. He can turn off the taps, flip off lights and other energy-using sources, put the trash where it belongs, and turn off the heat or air. Talk over each area of misuse. (1) Can he use less water when he showers or brushes his teeth? (2) Can he turn off lights and the television when he leaves a room? (3) Can he put litter in trash containers? (4) Can he put on a sweater when cold and take off more clothes when hot to use heating and cooling units less frequently? Reevaluate your own example in these areas.

WORD CONCEPTS *Concept Cards*

Objective: to visually clarify the special study words for the month.
Materials needed: scissors and the activity sheet (p. 89).

Cut the sheet along the lines into small cards. Shuffle and turn them upside down in a pile. Let the child pick a card one at a time and state whether he thinks the picture represents *few, many, fragile, unbreakable, sinking* or *floating*. Talk about each one.

PRE-MATH *Place Settings*

Objective: to allow the child to count out a predetermined number of objects and to feel the pride of fulfilling a difficult responsibility.

Let your child set the table for a meal.

Clarify how many people will be present and let him take it from there. He can count out plates, silver, cups, and napkins and put them neatly in their places. Praise him generously before the family at mealtime for a job well done.

PRE-READING *The Dictionary*

Objective: to review alphabetical order, to be impressed with the volume of words within the English language, and to identify familiar letters.

Materials needed: a dictionary.

Scan the dictionary together. Say the alphabet as you flip briskly through the pages to find the corresponding letters. Select a few letters to study in depth. Show your child how every word within each section begins with the same letter. Let your child point to the letter in the words he sees. Read several words that would be familiar to him. Can he think of what they mean? If the dictionary is illustrated, choose a couple of new words to introduce. The pictures will enhance your simplified descriptions.

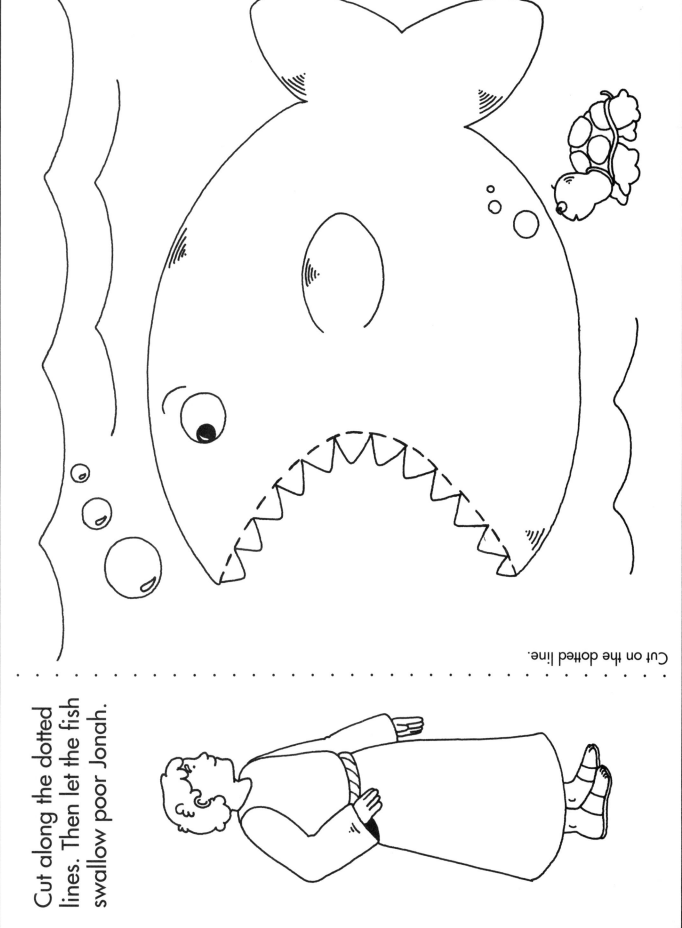

Cut on the dotted line.

Cut along the dotted lines. Then let the fish swallow poor Jonah.

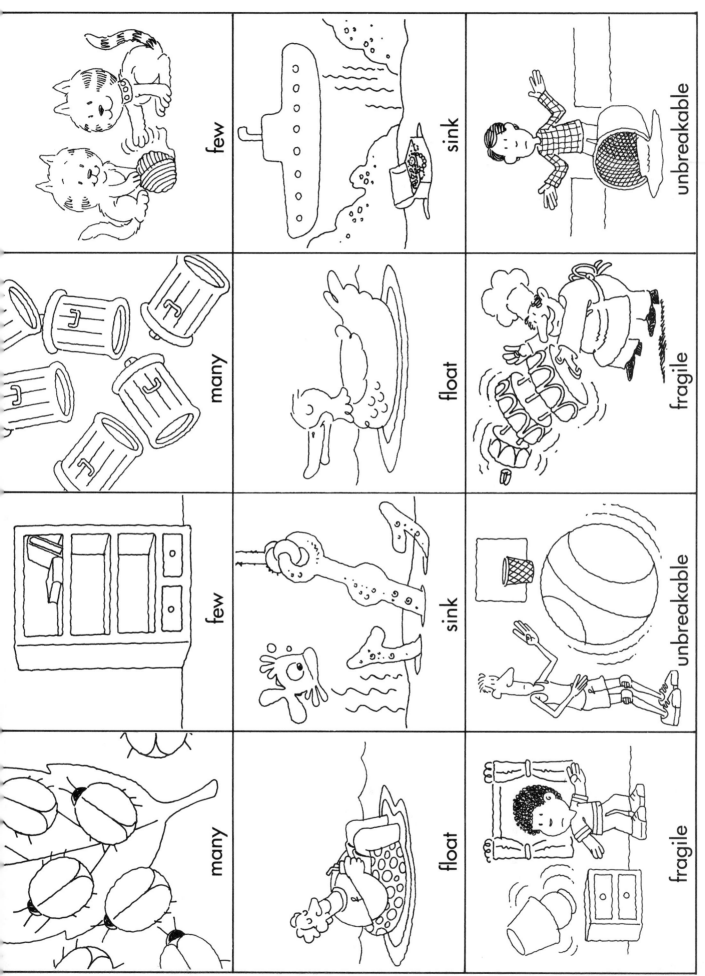

few

sink

unbreakable

many

float

fragile

few

sink

unbreakable

many

float

fragile

J U L Y

CHARACTER: fairness
OUR WORLD: communications
WORDS: over/under, top/bottom, front/back

As children, my brother and I loved to play Monopoly. David's strategy was to go for the big killing as the proprietor of a hotel along Boardwalk. I usually tried to nickel and dime him to death with the acquisition of two complete streets of low income property and the railroads. The game always got bogged down, however, when it came to undefined terms. How much should be in the pot for a landing on "Free Parking?" Do you get paid for passing "Go" when you're on your way to jail? How much interest can your opponent charge when offering a loan to keep you in the game? Without question, what I

thought was fair and equitable was a completely unsuitable compromise for my brother. We would spend hours dickering and fuming over unresolved conflicts. How much better would it have been if we had sat down before the game ever began and communicated. Without raising tempers and mid-game passion, it would have been easy to negotiate just and impartial solutions.

Thinking back on those feverish games, I see how communication could have greatly facilitated the implementation of fairness. Communication begets fairness. Thus we arrive at the two themes for this month. What a perfect chance for God to bring people and situations into your life to challenge you in these very areas. For example, consider becoming more adventurous in conversation. Are there ways to cut down on meaningless chitchat, allowing your soul to become a participant by exchanging real thoughts and ideas? Check out your dealings with family, friends, and co-workers. Do you deal impartially and equitably with all? No favorites and no hidden agendas? True teaching occurs when a life-change touches another life. This month will be a highlight for your child if it has become dynamic for you.

WEEK ONE

CHARACTER   *Good Sportsmanship*

Objective: to help the child realize that fairness means equal rules for himself and others.
Materials needed: two pieces of tissue paper.

Provide an opportunity for your child to experience both winning and losing by inventing a little contest. Place two crumpled pieces of tissue paper side by side at the end of a long table. Who will blow his paper to the other end first, parent or child? Watch and comment on the reaction of your child both when the game has gone well and when he couldn't beat his opponent. Move from your observations about the way he responded directly into the following story.

There once was a girl named Rachel who always did very well at whatever she tried. Her mommy and daddy would tell all the neighbors how well she knew her letters and numbers. They said she was even starting to learn how to read. She could already ride a bike, and she wasn't even in kindergarten yet.

But none of the other children on the block liked to play with Rachel. Their mothers would say, "Rachel is such a smart and pretty girl. Why don't you let her play in your games?" The children would just shake their heads and mutter something about not liking her.

The truth was that Rachel had never learned how to be fair. She hated to lose any game. If she was playing kickball, she would change the rules so that she always won. If she played hopscotch and jumped over the line, she would say, "No I didn't!" If she was playing with dolls, her dolls always got the first and the best of everything.

Poor Rachel never had any good friends, never got invited to spend the night, never made popcorn balls or ran through the sprinklers with the other children because she wasn't fun to be with. Rachel just wasn't fair.

OUR WORLD   *Verbal and Nonverbal Communication*

Objective: to introduce communication and consider its many facets.

Define *communication* for your child as "giving a message to someone else." Talk about all the ways this can be done . . . using telephone, TV, mail, books, radio, newspapers, art, music, the stage, etc. Visually illustrate as many of these mediums as possible by looking at an example of each and considering how it is used. Then sit down in chairs, facing one another and tell your child that you will communicate several messages without writing or using your voice. (Smile, tap your fingers, shake your head, yawn, clap your hands, wipe your eyes, gasp, etc.) After each nonverbal demonstration, ask what message was communicated.

WORD CONCEPTS   *Obstacle Course*

Objective: to experience each of this month's words for study in a hands-on way.
Materials needed: string.

Prepare a course to be followed throughout your house and yard by laying the string as a path to be followed. Let it run over the *top* of a bed, underneath the *bottom* of a table, *over* a bench, *under* a tree branch, around the *front* of a couch and the *back* of a chair, etc. Take your child over the route and explain each curve and meander, liberally using the words of the month. Time your child as he jockeys through the course.

PRE-MATH   *Picture Book*

Objective: to review numbers and numbering in a slightly different way.
Materials needed: a short picture book.

Allow your child to flip through the pages of the book and count all the illustrations that appear within its covers. For more challenge, give the child a page number and ask him to find the page and describe the picture that he finds there.

PRE-READING   *Bingo*

Objective: to promote visual recognition of alphabetical letters.
Materials needed: scissors, pennies, a bowl, and the activity sheet (p. 99).

Cut out the game boards and letter slips. Put the letters in a bowl and draw them out one at a time. Call out each letter as it is drawn and let the players put a penny on the corresponding letter on their own card. The child can play with a parent or a friend. The player who achieves a straight line vertically or horizontally calls out "Bingo" and wins the game. Even if the child is unable to identify all the letters on his card, he is learning recognition as the parent works with him.

W E E K   T W O

CHARACTER   *Restitution*

Objective: to point out that fairness involves restitution being made for every wrong, whenever possible.

Materials needed: pencil and the activity sheet (p. 101).

Tell the following story and then look at the activity sheet. Make up a short narrative to go with each picture on the left. Then let your child match it with the square on the right that shows a possible way to right the wrong. Let your child suggest what he would do in a similar circumstance.

Cindy tiptoed into her sister's bedroom. She tiptoed because she had a feeling that she shouldn't be there. Her older sister had gotten a new bottle of perfume and promised to let her have a little sniff. "Later," she had said. And now it was later and Cindy wanted to smell the beautiful smell.

"Oops!" she cried as she tripped over a shoe on the floor and crashed into the bureau. The long handled mirror, resting on the top, spun crazily around and crashed in pieces on the floor.

Later in her own room, she heard her sister cry, "What happened to my mirror?" The whole family trooped into her sister's bedroom and listened as Cindy confessed what she had done. She felt terrible!

Her dad put his arm around her shoulders. "We all know it was just an accident. So don't worry. But we also know that you came into your sister's room without permission. And of course the mirror is still broken. It must be paid for," he concluded.

Tears came into Cindy's eyes. "But how can I do that?" she asked.

"Well," her dad said thoughtfully. "We could provide some odd jobs around the house where you might be able to pick up a little money. And if you save it all, you'll soon be able to pay for a new mirror."

OUR WORLD   *Mailing a Letter*

Objective: to make use of one type of communication.
Materials needed: construction paper, markers, stickers (optional), an envelope, and a stamp.

Decide together on just the right person to receive a note from your child. Design a card with pictures and simple words. Help him with the letters as needed, but allow the rest to be his own creative accomplishment. Make sure a message of some sort is being communicated, whether it is love, good wishes, or a wish to see the recipient. Slip the card into an envelope, adorn with a stamp, and drop into a mailbox. Think about how the person will react when he receives the note. How will he feel?

WORD CONCEPTS   *Front and Back*

Objective: to provide sensory experiences to differentiate front from back.

Look at your own body. Which is the front and which is the back? If things were reversed, would you be able to see where you were going? Could you walk? Sit? Eat? How would your clothing fit? Try to put on a shirt, pair of pants, and socks with the backs in the front. Look in the mirror. Think of some other simple endeavors to try backwards. How can they be done?

PRE-MATH   *Collection Counting*

Objective: to give an opportunity to count and handle some cherished objects.
Materials needed: a collection of some sort.

If your child has a collection of anything (bottle caps, dolls, rocks, models, leaves, whatever), drag it out and count how many pieces he has in his possession. If he doesn't own a collection, perhaps it is time to begin assembling and hoarding some "treasures." Never eliminate this important part of a child's life for reasons of neatness or tidiness. Collections can be a basis for comparison as he notices similarities and disparities between items. Collections can provide many opportunities to count and recount. Collections can encourage observation skills as your child searches for valuables in unlikely places. Help your child to discover the best way to sort and display his collection.

PRE-READING   *TV Reporting*

Objective: to let your child practice formulating sentences that are grammatically correct and thematically oriented while emphasizing another aspect of communication.
Materials needed: a large box, markers, and scissors.

Help your child to think of some newsworthy items around your house (i.e. brother got a haircut, dog had a bath, a new flower bloomed). Prepare a news broadcast for which he is the anchorperson. Allow him to report the news over "TV" by cutting a square hole out of the front of the box, removing the back and decorating it with knobs and a speaker like a real set. If you have the time to do it up right, plan commercials, use a tape for introduction music, and let him perform what he has rehearsed for the family.

WEEK THREE

CHARACTER   *Fairness in Responsibility*

Objective: to establish the fairness of family demands and to show that maturity demands responsibility as well as privilege.
Materials needed: paper, stapler, and crayons.

Tell the following story and end it with a discussion about the dangers of making comparisons. Children are constantly contrasting their own responsibilities and privileges with other children. For example: "Jimmy's mommy bought him this toy. Why can't I have it too?"—or—"You always let Ruthie stay up late. Why can't I?"—or—"Why do I have to do this big job? Sally has only a little work."—or—"George gets to watch all the cartoons he wants to. Please let me watch TV!" Bring up any grievances previously expressed or let your child vent any "inequalities" he sees. Give your child reasons for any apparent unfairness. Work together on making a little notebook (picture pages stapled together) entitled, "I Am Big!" Your child can draw an illustration on each page of something he does today that he was too little to do a year ago.

"This package is too heavy," wailed Jeremy. "And my legs are too tired." He dropped the bag and flounced down on the sidewalk beside it.

"Oh, Jeremy," said his mother wearily. "Not here!" She had his baby sister in one arm and a bigger package in the other. With a huge sigh, Jeremy slowly trailed down the sidewalk toward the house. Once inside, his mother asked if he could start putting the groceries away as she headed off into the bedroom to put the baby down for a nap.

Jeremy obeyed, but he was upset. He muttered to himself, "That baby is nothing but trouble. I have to do all the work around here, and she's the one who gets all the attention. It's just not fair."

He had almost finished putting the last can away when his mom came into the room. He slammed the cupboard door. "All Melissa ever does is cry and eat. How come you always help her? I wish I could just play and lay around all day."

His mother smiled. "No you don't," she said gently. "You are older so you have more jobs and responsibilities. But you also have more special privileges. I was just going to thank you for helping me this morning and ask if you wanted to share a root beer float with me."

"Oh yeah!" shouted Jeremy. "I love those!"

"Of course if you'd rather, you may take a nap like Melissa," his mom teased.

OUR WORLD *Paper Cup Telephone*

Objective: to point out another avenue of communication.
Materials needed: scissors, string, and two paper cups.

Poke a hole in the bottom of each cup. Push the string through the hole from the outside to the inside and tie a knot so that it won't slip back through. Extend the cups apart so the line is somewhat taut and the string is not touching anything. Use this invention as you would a telephone. One person can speak into one cup while the other person listens to the transmitted voice in the other one. Emphasize that the telephone is one way that communication (the giving of messages) can be carried on. Now would be a good time to rehearse some basic phone manners.

WORD CONCEPTS *Which Half?*

Objective: to present the differences between a *top* and a *bottom*.
Materials needed: a piece of construction paper and fifteen to twenty small household items.

Using the construction paper as a barrier, conceal one item at a time from the view of your child. Let half of the object appear over the top of the paper. Let the child name the object and determine whether he is seeing the *top* or the *bottom* half of each. Is this information important to know?

PRE-MATH *Tracing*

Objective: to practice the skills involved in writing numbers.
Materials needed: pencil, marker, and lightweight paper.

With a marker and in bold print, sketch several numbers on a page. Place a light sheet of white paper on the first page and let your child trace the numbers you've drawn. Help him to know where to begin writing. Assist him in knowing if the pencil should remain on the page or be lifted and placed in a different spot in the middle of the number.

PRE-READING *Newspaper Letters*

Objective: to prove how the letters we study are used in very important places.

Materials needed: a newspaper and a marker.

Using the headlines or large print advertisements, thumb through the newspaper to spot some of the letters of the alphabet that your child knows. Take a bright marker and let your child circle them. Add some new letters to his repertoire. Read the more prominent headlines in which several letters were identified, to show that the letters really do form words. Talk about the newspaper as a vital form of communication in our country.

WEEK FOUR

CHARACTER *Being a Peacemaker*

Objective: to show how an arbitrator might arrive at a fair decision.

Materials needed: a doll (or favorite stuffed animal), a dull knife, construction paper, marker, and a safety pin.

Use the doll and the knife as an object lesson to illustrate the following story, based on 1 Kings 3:16-28, after it has been told. With many reassurances that you will not carry out your proposal, talk about how the child would feel to have his beloved toy cut in two. Think about the important role a peacemaker can play. Cut a round circle out of construction paper and write on the front, *I AM A PEACEMAKER.* Pin it on your child's shirt and think of ways for him to be fair around the home and neighborhood.

Solomon was a king with a very hard job. Whenever people in his kingdom got in trouble or didn't know what to do, they would come to him to make it right. He would have to fix their problems and always be perfectly fair.

One day, two women came to him who were arguing and very upset. They were carrying a baby and each of them said the baby was her baby! What was King Solomon going

to do? He must be perfectly fair. But how could he tell who was telling the truth? Whose baby was it?

King Solomon was very wise. So he worked out a plan. He had a big soldier come in with a knife and say he was going to cut the baby in half. Then the women would not have to argue, each one could have a piece of the baby for her own. (Solomon would never really cut the baby in half, but his plan worked just the way he wanted it to.)

The woman who was just pretending that the baby was hers said, "OK, cut the baby in half." She didn't really care about the baby, she just didn't want the other lady to get him.

The real mother was horrified. "Oh no!" she said, for she really loved her child. "It would be much better if the other lady took my baby than have the poor child cut in two."

Then Solomon knew who the real mommy was, so he sent the bad woman away. He gave the baby back to his real mother. Solomon had been perfectly fair.

OUR WORLD *Codes*

Objective: to experience the difficulty of communicating without words.

Materials needed: four sheets of paper, four sticks, and cellophane tape.

Tape the paper to the sticks to make flags. Think of some simple signals to use with the flags in your hands. Arms up could be yes. Arms down, no. Arms extended, all's well. Waving could be asking for help. After defining these and other messages, try to communicate to one another across a field or yard. See if you can make your thoughts be seen and received. Talk afterward about any confusion and how it could have been avoided.

WORD CONCEPTS *Scavenger Hunt*

Objective: to encourage the child to know and apply the words of the month.

Materials needed: six small household items, paper, and a pencil.

Before the game begins, number a sheet from one to six. Next to each number draw a simple picture of one of the items that you have selected to use for the game. This will serve as a list of objects for the child to find in the hunt. Use each of the special words of the month when deciding where to hide an object. For example: put a spoon in *back* of the piano, a pencil *under* the chair, a coin on *top* of the bureau, etc. Give your child the pictured list of items and let the hunt begin. If hints are necessary, use the words you want to enforce to describe the places where the items are hidden.

PRE-MATH *Following Number Directions*

Objective: to relate a verbal number with a visual amount and to review the many ways to communicate.

Materials needed: a pen and the activity sheet (p. 103).

Ask the child to add the following things to the picture on the activity sheet:

1. nine pushbuttons on the phone
2. three more books on the shelves
3. two pictures on the wall
4. five more pencils in the cup
5. one newspaper in the man's hands
6. five dials on the radio
7. six squares on the TV screen
8. one smile on the man's face

Discuss all the ways a person can communicate as pictured on the page.

PRE-READING *Fine Art*

Objective: to catch the spirit of an artist and what he wanted to communicate, while furthering pre-reading skills.

Sit down in front of a detailed painting or picture in your home (or selected from a book). Talk about what the artist might have been trying to communicate. Look for details. Name the objects you recognize. Can you child state what letter each object starts with? Work together on hearing and identifying beginning sounds.

S	L	G	M
R	P	H	U
K	D	X	Z
I	Y	J	E

Cut out the two boards

Y	D	E	J
U	X	S	Z
G	M	I	K
P	R	L	H

Cut apart

S	M
Z	Y
H	J
K	P
U	X
D	E
G	I
L	R

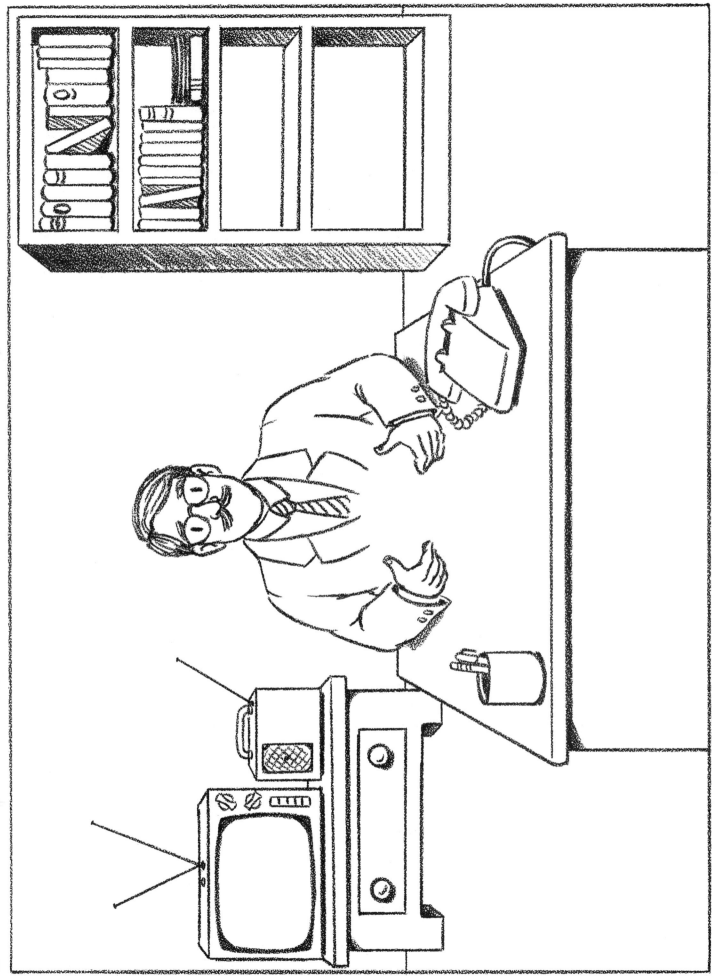

CHARACTER: discretion

OUR WORLD: myself

WORDS: safe/dangerous, thick/thin, strong/weak

I watched little Johnnie sitting stiffly in the hardback Sunday School chair. Every hair on his head was regimented into proper place and a bow tie was tightly fastened to the collar at his neck. I could almost read his thoughts as he reviewed his mother's last whispered warnings: "Be good. Don't talk. Sit still. And put your offering in when the plate is passed." But did she know a fly was going to land on his nose? He discreetly blew it away. But it immediately zoomed back with the defiance of a dive bomber. The hand clutching his offering nickel hesitantly waved. By now the fly was circling, insistent-ly making pass after pass. Without turning his head, he followed its flight with his eyes. At last it landed on the head of the child directly in front of him. In an act of final desperation, he held his Bible high in the air and brought it down sturdily over the head of the unsuspecting pupil just in front of him.

"I can't figure out what got into him," the teacher said after class to Johnnie's mother. "I've never seen him act that way before!"

Our character quality of discretion intro-duces the child to the proper times and places to speak and act. Do you allow your child loud and rowdy times to offset the occasions when social etiquette is desired? Have you ever defined the difference between one type of setting (with its accompanying requirements) and another?

The second topic for exploration is entitled "Myself." It takes the theme of discretion and broadens it to cover more than just teaching your child how to handle himself. He will learn all about who he is, his five senses, how to be healthy, and what to do with emotions. What a special time to express how important your child has become to you!

WEEK ONE

CHARACTER *Mephibosheth*

Objective: to introduce the thought that there are appropriate actions to correspond with specific times.

Tell the following story from 2 Samuel 4:4 and 9:1-13, with a discussion about certain people that need extra loving treatment. Around whom would it be important to act quietly, calmly, and gently? Talk about what actions would assist or alarm an older person, a baby, or a person with a particular disability. Set up a role play situation in which you pretend to be a senior citizen. Let your child practice appropriate behavior.

King Saul had a grandson named Mephibosheth. He was a prince in the palace with his father Jonathan. But one day, both his father and grandfather were killed in battle. He was only five years old. The nurse that was caring for him feared the enemy would come and kill little Mephibosheth. She grabbed the boy in her arms and started to run with him to safety. But in her hurry, she dropped him. His legs were badly hurt, and he never walked again.

The next king to take the throne was Da-

vid. Years passed before David found out that one of Saul's grandsons was still living. He ordered Mephibosheth (now a grown man), to come before him. Mephibosheth was afraid that David would kill him as many other kings in his place might have done. So he threw himself down at David's feet and said, "Sir, I am ready to be your servant."

David was a good-hearted king though. The first thing he said to the crippled man was, "Don't be afraid." He felt love for Mephibosheth. He told him he could eat every meal at a special table in the palace, just like one of his own sons. He gave him back the land that had belonged to his grandfather Saul.

Even though David was a strong and tough warrior who killed thousands of men in battle, he knew that there were times to be gentle and kind.

OUR WORLD *Dodge Ball*

Objective: to see and know essential body parts.
Materials needed: a ball that is soft.

Review all the basic parts of your child's body before beginning the game. To play, one person puts his back against a wall. The other person stands behind a given line and attempts to throw the ball and hit the first player. The players then exchange places. Try this game with one variation. When one player hits the other player with the ball, he must name the part of the body that has been struck.

WORD CONCEPTS *Vanilla Pudding*

Objective: to see the contrast between *thick* and *thin* and to experience a substance that demands all five senses.
Materials needed: two quart saucepan, ½ cup sugar, 2 Tbs. cornstarch, ⅛ tsp. salt, 2 cups milk, 2 egg yolks (beaten slightly), 2 Tbs. softened margarine, and 2 tsps. vanilla.

Make vanilla pudding as follows: blend sugar, starch, and salt in a pan. Combine milk and egg yolks, then stir into the first mixture. Cook over medium heat until substance boils. Let boil for one more minute, stirring constantly. Remove from heat and stir in the margarine and vanilla. Chill. As you cook, contrast the ingredients that were used to make the pudding (milk, eggs, softened margarine, and vanilla) with the finished result. Were the ingredients *thin* in nature? How did the pudding end up so *thick?* Make use of each of your child's five senses. Point out the part of his body that is perceiving: eyes, nose, ears, mouth, or hands. Let him see the various ingredients, smell the vanilla, hear the sound of the thickened mixture boiling, feel the difference between thick and thin, and taste the cooled pudding. For the ultimate sensory experience, pour some of the mixture onto the counter top, and let him finger paint as he eats.

PRE-MATH   *What's Wrong?*

Objective: to cause the child to count and compare numbers that are not the same.
Materials needed: activity sheet (p. 113).

Take a look at the strange creature in the accompanying illustration. Study every body part. Have your child count its members. Compare with his own body parts. Are they the same? What advantages would the monster creature have over a human? Is there anything that your child could do better with his own body?

PRE-READING   *Name Plate*

Objective: to practice shaping the letters that make up your child's name.
Materials needed: cardboard, glue, yarn, paint, brush, and a pencil.

Work on a plaque for the door of your child's room. Use an appropriate sized piece of cardboard as the background. Help your child to write the letters of his name on the cardboard. Add an apostrophe with an *s.* Just beneath the name, write the word *ROOM.* Trace the lines with glue. Add a border in glue around the edge. Follow the pattern you have made in glue with the yarn to make three dimensional letters. After the glue has dried, paint the whole surface a solid color. Mount on your child's door.

WEEK TWO

CHARACTER   *Definition of Discretion*

Objective: to learn in an indelible way what discretion means.

After telling the following story, repeat Mortimer's definitions for your child. Let him say it back to you until he knows it well. Throughout the day, prod his memory with a quick quiz: "Do you remember what discretion means?"

My name is Mortimer. I am a very handsome mouse. I have the most beautiful set of whiskers that you have ever seen. I brush them out in front of the mirror every morning. Believe it or not, I'm even smarter than I am good looking! I know some big words that some human people don't even know—like "discretion." Do you know what that means? I didn't think so. Discretion is knowing the proper time and place for everything. Hey! I'm just a mouse, but even I know not to run across the middle of the floor in broad daylight. I carefully wait until it is dark before I come out on my cheese raids.

I want to tell you about a little boy named Brian who lives in the same house I do. Do you think he knows what discretion means? No way! You ought to hear the unbelievable noise he makes while his mother is on the phone. Discretion means knowing when it is time to be quiet. One time his sister wanted to give her dad a present. Guess who blabbed what it was before Dad even got to open it. Brian did! Discretion means knowing how to keep a secret until it's the right time to tell. I'd sure hate to go to church with him. I'll bet he doesn't know that discretion means to sit still and keep quiet so that everybody can hear about God.

Don't get me wrong! It's not that I don't know how to have fun. You ought to see some of the parties that I throw down in my little mouse hole. Me and my friends play "Pin the tail on the Cat" and "Blind Mouse Bluff." We squeak and scurry around, making all kinds of rumpus. But when daylight comes, I don't want to scare the humans, so I'm as quiet as a . . . well, you know, quiet as a mouse.

Brian now, he needs to learn from me. He can yell and scream all he wants—in his room during playtime. He can throw a ball all over the place—in the yard. He can climb and crawl anywhere he likes—in the tree in the backyard. That's discretion. Knowing when and where to do everything. And don't you ever forget who told you all about it. Me . . . Mortimer the mouse!

OUR WORLD Puppet Show

Objective: to show that manners make another person more important than yourself.
Materials needed: two teacups and two puppets (or stuffed animals).

Use the puppets to introduce the topic of manners. Let one figure represent improper decorum. The second figure should present a contrast through good behavior. The setting is a tea party. The uncultured puppet puts his elbows on the table, talks with his mouth full, interrupts when others are talking, plays with his food, burps, and acts in a rude manner. The second puppet is careful to make proper introductions, passes the food to others first, speaks quietly, uses his utensils the way they were meant to be used, asks to be excused, and conducts himself in a polite and civilized way.

After the skit, talk about what has been learned and how to incorporate it. Explain that a child with manners will treat others in a considerate and selfless way.

OUR WORLD Doll Bath

Objective: to give indirect pointers to the child on keeping his body clean.
Materials needed: doll, washcloth, towel, shampoo, soap, toothbrush, toothpaste, and a hairbrush.

Prepare a bath for the doll. Show your child how to keep a body clean by using the doll as the demonstration model. Let the child perform as many of these functions as he can. Scrub the skin with the washcloth, lather all the hard to remember places and rinse well. Wash, dry, and brush the doll's hair. Help the doll to put on clean clothing. Talk about between bath cleanliness. When should the doll remember to wash her hands and face? How should nails be cared for? How should the toothbrush be used?

PRE-MATH Exercise Course

Objective: to enforce the visual appearance of each number and its sequential order.
Materials needed: ten sheets of construction paper and a marker.

Number the construction paper pages from one to ten. Plan an exercise course around your house and yard. At each stop, hang up one of the numbers you have drawn so the child can follow the course in sequence. Each station should require a different activity corresponding to the number posted: one chin up, two somersaults, three skips with a jump rope, four push-ups, five jogs in place, etc. The parent can state what calistenics to perform. After you have completed the course together, talk about the benefits of exercise. How does working out produce healthy bodies?

PRE-READING Clothing Tags

Objective: to give another source of reading material and to prove the importance of letters and numbers.

Look together at the tags on the clothes your child is wearing. What does S, M, L, and

XL mean? Check out the numbers that tell the size. Rummage through drawers and closet for clothing that has become too small. Compare the labels with those that are yet too big. What letters and numbers appear on mom's and dad's clothes?

WEEK THREE

CHARACTER *Overindulgence*

Objective: to clarify that discretion knows when to stop and never does anything in excess.

Relate the following story, asking these questions at the end:

(1) What happens when you eat too much candy?

(2) What happens when you play at the beach without protection from the sun?

(3) What happens when you get out more than one puzzle at a time?

(4) What happens when you turn a radio on as loud as it will go?

(5) What happens when you mix every color of paint together?

(6) What happens when you sit in one position for a very long time?

(7) What happens when you sit too close to a fireplace?

(8) What happens when you ride too fast on a bike?

(9) What happens when you lift something too heavy for you?

(10) What happens when you put too much of one ingredient in a recipe?

Clarify with each question that too much of any one thing (no matter how nice it is) is never good. Discretion tells you when to stop.

When the Children of Israel were traveling through the desert, they had no food to eat. God wanted them to pray to Him for every-thing that they needed. One of the things He prepared for them was a light, flaky bread that fell from the sky every night. The first time the people saw it they cried, "Manna!" Manna means, "What is it?" That name stuck. They called it manna ever after.

But there were some rules that went with this free food from heaven. When families went out each day to gather manna for their meals, they were to gather only what they needed. No more, no less. If they didn't pick enough, they would grow hungry. If they hoarded too much, the manna would turn bad and get worms. God wanted to teach His people discretion. He wanted them to learn how much was just right.

Later the people grew tired of eating only manna. They began to ask for meat to eat. God answered their request by sending a whole flock of low-flying quail. The people could grab the birds right out of the sky. Now they had tons of meat. They were so greedy that they ate and ate and ate. They ate so much it practically came out their ears and noses. The Bible says they got sick to death of quail. They had not learned to use discretion. They did not know when to stop.

OUR WORLD *Making Cookies*

Objective: to provide a forum of discussion about diet and what is healthy or harmful for your body.

Materials needed: 1 cup margarine, $1/2$ cup honey, 1 cup corn syrup, 1 egg, 1 tsp. vanilla, 1-$1/2$ cups flour, 1 tsp. baking soda, $3/4$ tsp. salt, 3 cups rolled oats, and raisins.

Make cookies together while discussing the detriments of processed foods, high sugar and salt intakes, additives, and too much cholesterol. Contrast these substitutes with natural ingredients, wholesome fruits and vegetables, and hearty grains that build strong, active bodies.

Beat the margarine, corn syrup, and honey together until light and fluffy. Beat in the egg and vanilla. Combine flour, baking soda, and salt. Add to the first mixture. Stir in the oats.

Drop rounded teaspoonfuls onto an ungreased cookie sheet. Bake 10 minutes in a 350 degree oven. Enjoy!

WORD CONCEPTS *Driving a Nail*

Objective: to provide a method of measuring *strength* and *weakness*.
Materials needed: a board, a hammer, and nails.

With your child, take a look at his muscles in the mirror. If he were a farmer accustomed to lifting heavy hay bales, what muscles would bulge? If he were a cross country skier, would different muscles be strong? How about a pianist, or a cowboy, or a carpenter? See for yourself what muscles are involved in driving a nail. Have a contest to see who can pound the nail completely into the wood first. Who is *weak* and who is *strong?*

PRE-MATH *Catalog People*

Objective: to provide another whole realm for categorizing and counting.
Materials needed: clothing catalogs, cardboard, scissors, and glue.

Mount the figures of some average-sized people from the catalog with glue onto the cardboard. Cut the cardboard to match their body shapes. Look with your child through the rest of the catalog to find different clothes for the cardboard people to wear. Cut out the clothing, leaving several tabs along the side to fold over the cardboard figures to keep the clothes in place. Choose a whole wardrobe for the men and women paper dolls to wear. Count the various pieces of apparel that you have selected. How many are for warm weather? How many for cold? How many blue? How many red?

PRE-READING *Personal Hygiene Chart*

Objective: to provide letter practice while encouraging personal cleanliness habits.
Materials needed: a pencil and the activity sheet (p. 115).

Work together on completing the activity sheet. Start by determining the beginning sound of each word. What letter goes with that sound? What does it look like? Practice writing it out before putting it in the blank. After the page is finished, show your child how the chart can be used every day.

WEEK FOUR

CHARACTER *Still Life*

Objective: to visually implant a verse of Scripture through a graphic illustration.
Materials needed: paint, paintbrush, paper, a bowl of apples, and a decorative frame.

Artistically arrange a bowl of apples and a picture frame to be the subject of a still life for your child to paint. Before he begins, help him to capture an imaginative glimpse at "apples of gold in settings of silver." As he works on portraying the magic of that phrase, learn Proverbs 25:11 together. Why is a word "aptly spoken" like a beautiful still life? What are some gracious and uplifting things to say to people? Does a person with discretion say the right thing at the right time?

OUR WORLD *Private Places*

Objective: to open conversation about personal body parts and the importance of keeping them private.

After telling the following story, talk seriously to your child about the parts of his body that are meant to be kept private. Talk about what behavior by another person should put him on guard and what to do if anyone ever tries to violate him. Use the following story as a springboard to assure the child that he need not ever reveal what is personal. Something that is private belongs to the owner alone.

Bill had a special place to play. It was a refrigerator box almost completely hidden in the corner of the yard. It was the only place he could go to be totally alone. It was surrounded by bushes and was the closest thing to a pirate's hideout that you ever saw.

Bill's mom and dad were the only ones that knew about his secret clubhouse. He made them promise not to tell a soul. Even Scott, his best buddy from next door wasn't allowed. But just in case a snoopy sister or uninvited squirrel should stumble onto his secret, he decided to make a sign. His mom helped him with the spelling, but he did it mostly himself. In big, bold letters the sign said, "PRIVATE! KEEP OUT!" That meant that no one but Bill could enter. Period.

One night, after he had securely attached the sign to the door of his hideout, he decided to rummage through the attic to find some more treasures to stow in his pirates lair. He had just found a pair of old boots that might come in handy, when his eye caught some lettering that looked very familiar. The word was fixed firmly to the drawer of a battered looking file cabinet. Where had he seen that before? In a flash he remembered! The word was *private*. The same word he had painted on the sign that was now plastered over the door of his own hideout. He knew exactly what it meant. Whatever was in that file cabinet was not for just anyone to see. It was personal. Meant only for whoever owned it.

By now he was really curious. What could be so important in that drawer? Surely it wouldn't hurt to take a teeny tiny peek. Very slowly Bill opened the drawer an inch. Nothing popped out. All was quiet. Finally, he took a deep breath and opened it all the way. How disappointing! All he saw was a stack of musty old papers. He was just leafing through the ones in the very front hoping to find a treasure map or something equally exciting, when a loud slam startled him so much that he tore the page he was holding. White and trembling, he whipped around to see his father standing in the door. The half torn sheet was still in Bill's hand.

"I just came to call you to dinner," his father said. "Sorry I startled you. This old door keeps sticking and I really had to shove to get it open. By the way, what is that you're holding?" With downcast eyes, Bill showed his dad the paper that he had ripped.

After studying it for a moment, his dad asked where he had gotten it. Bill pointed toward the file. "Bill, you should never have been in that drawer," his dad said as seriously as Bill had ever seen him. "Those are important documents that are filed in a certain order. By thumbing through them you may have gotten the papers out of sequence and now I shall have to send to a government office to have the torn one replaced. Don't you know what the word *private* means?"

Bill felt ashamed. He knew exactly what *private* meant. He had put that word on the door of his clubhouse. Private meant to keep out. To stay away. Only certain people should see and know. The people to whom it belonged. "I'm sorry, Dad," he said.

WORD CONCEPTS *Safety Check*

Objective: to be able to see potential danger and learn the safe thing to do.

Take an instructional walk around the house. Stop at significant checkpoints to appraise items and situations that are potentially dangerous. For example, look into your medicine cabinet and warn your child of the risk in taking any substance without parental consent. Point out several electrical outlets and talk about what could happen if the child touched or meddled with the plugs and cords. Consider fireplaces and ovens and the possible hazard of fire and/or getting burned. Demonstrate how a toy left out could trip or injure someone. Take a peek into the garage, noticing tools with potential for harm. Review and rehearse planned family emergency procedures in case of fire, tornado, or earthquake. Mentally prepare your child for possible disaster, instilling not fear but confidence in knowing just what to do.

PRE-MATH *Dressing Race*

Objective: to see that time follows numerical sequences.

Pick out as many different styles of clothing as your child owns with various types of closures . . . buttons, snaps, ties, hooks, velcro, buckles, and zippers. Let your child race against the clock to put all the clothes on. (Assist him when necessary.) Count slowly out loud, so that he is aware of the passing of time. Liberally praise his efforts. Point out where the hand began on the clock and its movement until the task was completed. See if your child can beat his own time working backward to get all the items off.

PRE-READING *Cartoon Letters*

Objective: to hear the sounds that several alphabetical letters represent and to associate them with their written counterpart.

Materials needed: scissors, glue, and the activity sheet (p. 117).

Cut out the letters and see if the child can imagine the sound that each cartoon character might be uttering. Glue the appropriate letter inside the conversational bubble to which it belongs. Talk about all the different emotions that a person can feel. Which are expressed in the pictures? How does a child deal with what he feels inside?

August 1

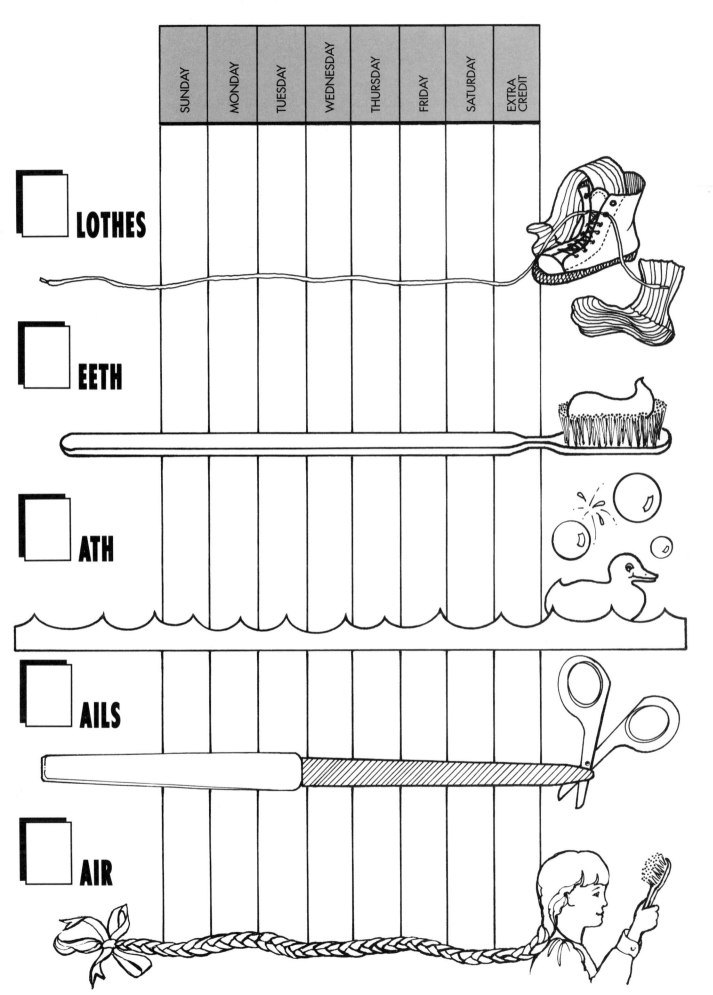

	SUNDAY	MONDAY	TUESDAY	WEDNESDAY	THURSDAY	FRIDAY	SATURDAY	EXTRA CREDIT

LOTHES

EETH

ATH

AILS

AIR

August 2

S E P T E M B E R

| CHARACTER: obedience |
| OUR WORLD: family |
| WORDS: right/left, up/down, above/below |

We swung the car into a gas station hoping desperately to find a knowledgeable attendant. Maybe he could decipher the map my friend had hurriedly scribbled the other day. Poring for the hundredth time over the microscopic scrap onto which the directions were traced, I reviewed my every turn up to this point. It seemed as if we had taken every step as indicated on our map. But the fact remained . . . we were at least three miles beyond our destination and hopelessly confused.

I rolled down the window and forlornly handed the map to the man at the pump. It took only a few minutes of study before he handed the paper back with a grin. In a few short sentences, the puzzle was explained and we were on our way. I had turned on "Capital Blvd." instead of waiting for "Capital Street."

The problem was twofold. First, I had to understand the directions and then I had to do what they said. Obedience within the framework of the family works the same way. Are you certain that when you give instructions they are clear, concise, and well defined? Have you taught your child to respond to your requests cheerfully and to the best of his ability? Obedience is just one dimension of family life, the other topic for this month. Looking at the family from the child's vantage point, we will seek to answer the following: How can family members learn to build up and strengthen one another? What are the inherent responsibilities and privileges of belonging? How can a child experience a true sense of heritage from the development of extended family relations?

I finally did find the way to the house of my friend. As I pulled into the drive, I saw a wave at the window. A moment later, the door of the house swung wide with welcome. The warm greeting I received was well worth the struggle to attain. And so it is within your own family. Your child will soon discover that the value of the home is well worth the exertion of obedience.

WEEK ONE

CHARACTER *Story of Balaam*

Objective: to define obedience as doing what you are told, when you are told, and without complaint.
Materials needed: crayon and the activity sheet (p. 127).

Tell the following story, found in Numbers 22:1-34, then work on the maze together. Talk about how Balaam should have responded to God, what God knew that the prophet didn't, how children should respond to their parents, and what parents know that children don't.

Balaam was a prophet of God. That meant that God would often use Balaam as His own messenger to tell the Children of Israel what they needed to know. But the enemies of God's people wanted to use Balaam also. They wanted him to say hurtful things. They came to the prophet's house and knocked on the door. "Balaam!" they called. "Look at all of the wonderful things we brought you." They showed him beautiful clothes, lots of money, and flashy jewelry. "All you have to do to get these gifts is to go with us and say bad things about the Children of Israel," he was told.

Balaam wanted those beautiful prizes more than you could ever imagine. But he already knew what God would think about the awful things he was supposed to say. "Give me some time to think it over," he told the men. "I'll let you know tomorrow morning."

That night he talked to the Lord in prayer. "Please, please, please," he begged. "I know you don't want me to do it, but I do love all the presents they brought. A few bad words couldn't hurt anyone, could they?" God firmly told him no. It would not be right to hurt all of the nation of Israel just so that Balaam could get a few small gifts that he really wanted.

The next morning Balaam sadly sent the men from the enemy nation back to their homes. But not for long. Soon they were back with even more beautiful and expensive presents. They made the same offer. All Balaam had to do was go with them and say a few words and the gifts would all be his. Again the prophet hesitated. Instead of instant obedience to what he knew the Lord wanted, Balaam wanted to do things his own way. "Give me another night to think it over," he told the men."

That night he went back to the Lord in prayer. He began to whine and nag. Finally the Lord let him have what he wanted, but only to teach him a lesson. Balaam was thrilled. He ran to the men. "I can go! I can go!" he told them.

He hopped on his donkey and started out for the appointed place. On the way he had to travel down a narrow path with a rock wall on either side. But the donkey was acting very strangely. He kept stopping and flinching and charging into first one wall and then the other. Balaam began to get very angry.

What was wrong with that fool donkey! He hit the animal with a whip. Finally the donkey just lay down with the prophet still on his back. Then the Lord let the donkey speak. "Why are you hitting me? What have I done to you?" it said.

"You have disobeyed me. If I had a sword in my hand, I would kill you!" Balaam shouted. He had completely forgotten that he had done no better. He had not listened to the Lord's directions and had pushed for his own way as well.

Then the Lord let Balaam see why the donkey had acted so strangely. There was an angel with a great sword in his hand standing right in the middle of the path. If the donkey had not seen the angel and stopped, Balaam would have been killed. For the first time, he realized how foolish he had been to argue with God. Now Balaam was ready to obey. He fell flat on his face and said, "I'll go back home if you want me to."

OUR WORLD   *Family Tree*

Objective: to give your child a sense of belonging and heritage.
Materials needed: family photo album.

Use photographs to review your child's descendents. Don't get lengthy, just try to give him a panoramic view of all his loving family at once. Clarify who is related to whom. Punctuate your narrative with stories and funny tales about aunts, uncles, and great-grandparents. Tell who the child looks like (i.e.: you have a nose just like your uncle Ben).

WORD CONCEPTS   *Piñata*

Objective: to see a visual demonstration of the concepts *up* and *down*.
Materials needed: broom, string, paper bag, shredded newspaper, goodies (peanuts, candies, prizes, etc.), and a bat (or stick).

Tie a paper bag filled with shredded newspaper and goodies to one end of a broom. Hold the other end and use the broom as a boom to raise and lower the paper bag. Find a location well away from anything destructible, for the child will be trying to break open the bag with the bat. Make the target harder to hit by raising and lowering the piñata. Refer to its movement by calling out *up* and *down*.

PRE-MATH   *Counting Windows and Doors*

Objective: to reinforce the counting process and to compare larger and smaller numbers.

Walk around the house and have the child count all the doors. Walk around again and count all the windows. Compare the numbers. Were there more doors or windows?

PRE-READING   *Salt Letters*

Objective: to review several letters and to practice forming them.
Materials needed: salt.

Spill some salt onto a smooth surface like a table top. Use your pointer finger to form alphabetical letters in the white crystals. Work particularly on differentiating between similar but not identical letters, like *d* and *b*; *g*, *p*, and *q*; *m* and *n*; *i* and *l*.

WEEK TWO

CHARACTER   *Clothespin Family*

Objective: to realize the responsibilities of an authority figure as well as to determine the importance of instant and uncomplaining obedience.
Materials needed: one clothespin for each member of the family, construction paper, and glue.

Personify each clothespin with an identifiable trait. For example, if the dad in your family typically wears ties, use the construction paper to cut out and glue a miniature tie on the clothespin that will represent Dad. Perhaps add a baseball cap for brother, earrings for mom, and pigtails on sis. Let your child have a turn at manning each of the different figures to allow him to play out roles to which he is not accustomed. The parent can play whatever characters are left. Set out the following scenarios and see what action takes place. Use this as a learning experience centered around the concept of obedience. What difficulties does the person in charge have to face? What are the consequences of disobedience? How does the whole family benefit from the obedience of one child?

(1) Dad has given one of the children a job that is too hard for him to manage.

(2) A child in the family did not get enough sleep the night before and is very cranky.

(3) Mom is busy in the yard and has left an older child in charge of a younger child. The older child is too bossy and the younger child refuses to cooperate.

(4) Mom did not know that Dad already said the children could have no more cookies. One of the children asked Mom for a cookie and she said, "Yes."

(5) Mom has a big job helping some needy people in the community. Her work for them is not done, the children are hungry for lunch, and she asks for some help.

OUR WORLD *Special Sign*

Objective: to realize the importance of a loving family's support.

Develop a special sign to be an exclusive way for the members of your family to say "I love you" to each other. Let the child be in on the conceptualizing. Keep it simple and nonverbal so that whatever the occasion, the reassurance can still be subtly communicated. For example, your secret signal might be three hand squeezes, a tongue in the cheek or a double blink. Use it often over the next few days to establish it as a habit. Talk about when a person would especially appreciate a

message like that. Would it help to know that someone loves you when you are afraid, sick, late, tired, etc.?

WORD CONCEPTS *Habitats*

Objective: to delineate the meaning of *above* and *below* while affirming what is typically found in the land, sea, and sky.
Materials needed: a large sheet of paper and crayons.

Divide the paper in quarters by drawing a line horizontally and another vertically through the center of the page. Let the left half represent sky and sea and the right half sky and land. Lightly color each section. The sky can be blue, the land brown, and the water a deep blue. Give your child a list of items (one at a time), and let him draw each in its native habitat. Does the creature or object belong *above* the water or *under* the water; *above* the land or *under* the land? Help your child to picture the following on his paper in their rightful places: a worm, house, fish, sea gull, miner, plane, submarine, cloud, mole, kite, octopus, boat, etc.

PRE-MATH *Bottle Bowling*

Objective: to prompt the child to excel in addition as he scores in an exciting game.
Materials needed: several empty plastic liter bottles (or similar type container), a ball, paper, and pencil.

Set up the bottles at one end of a room. (A hallway might be best where an errant ball will cause little damage.) Take turns rolling the ball to see how many pins you can knock down. The academics become involved in the scoring portion of the game. Keep a running record on the paper of the scores, with marks or numbers to see who is currently ahead.

PRE-READING *Letter Puzzles*

Objective: to note specific characteristics about certain letters and to be able to identify them.

Materials needed: five pieces of one color construction paper, markers, and scissors.

Draw a letter of the alphabet on each of the five sheets of paper in thick, bold lines. Cut each page into three strips. At the beginning of the teaching session, lay the pages on the floor intact. Study the letters' features and talk about their names and sounds. Scramble the strips within each individual letter and let your child assemble it again. If that task was not too formidable, try mixing all the strips of every letter together and then putting them back in the right order.

W E E K   T H R E E

CHARACTER *Time for Dinner*

Objective: to show that obedience is more than just casually wishing to please, it is a commitment.

Tell the following story. Finish with a study of the clock. Look carefully at its face. Can your child identify any of the numbers on its surface? Show him the difference between an hour and minute hand. See if he can learn to identify the hour. Ask a few questions, such as: "If Mom says to be home at two, what time should you be home?" — and — "If Mom says to be home at three, what time should you be at home?"

Sharon had a best friend. She was one year older than Sharon and lived next door. Sometimes Sharon's mother would let her go play with her friend when her friend got home from school, but usually they just stayed at Sharon's house and played in the backyard or with the toys in her room. That way her mommy could keep an eye on her because she was the littlest.

One day Sharon's mother taught her to read a clock and tell time. Once she understood it, it was easy. Now she could visit her friend's house more often because she could tell what time she ought to be home.

The next day her friend asked her over. "Can I go and play next door?" Sharon asked her mother.

"Yes, but you must be home in one hour because that's the time for dinner," her mother said.

"OK!" Sharon hollered over her shoulder as she rushed out the door. She loved to play next door because her friend had a whole bedroom full of beautiful dolls. Soon she was busy giving them tea parties and taking them on walks. One time she looked up at the clock. Only five more minutes to play! It seemed like she had just gotten there. In a moment she forgot all about the time because one of her babies got sick, and she had to put it to bed.

Just then her friend's mommy walked into the room. "Your mother's on the phone," she said to Sharon.

"I'm sorry, Mommy!" she cried into the phone as she looked at the clock and saw she was already a half an hour late. "I'll be right home. I just forgot what time it was."

"That's OK, honey," said her mommy. "But I guess you also forgot that your Uncle Larry and Aunt Linda were going to be here for dinner. We began without you. I'm afraid we're almost through. You're going to have to learn this lesson the hard way."

OUR WORLD *Heirloom Hunt*

Objective: to place value on a family's heritage and to review some basic numerals.
Materials needed: paper, pencil, scissors, and an object from past generations.

Set up a treasure hunt to find a family heirloom. Number each clue and plan for one to lead to another. The parent will have to read the hints, but the child can certainly try to identify the numbers on the top of each paper. The clues might read as follows: "find the next clue under the piece of furniture that you sleep on." — or — "Under the tree is clue number three." End up with the discovery of the heirloom. It need not be expensive or elegant, just something to give them a feel for their predecessors and a sense of belonging. Tell the history of the item in a thrilling way. Then put it carefully away for safekeeping.

WORD CONCEPTS *Marching Orders*

Objective: to learn an automatic response to *right* and *left* instructions.

Review with the child which hand is his right and which is his left. Think of an easily identifiable reminder. Does he usually handle a spoon with his right hand? Does he prefer one hand over another when drawing? Use this as a reference point. Don hats, play imaginary instruments, carry banners, and construct your own parade. Call out instructions like a drill sergeant, with a special emphasis on the *"right* face" and *"left* face."

PRE-MATH *Laundry Line*

Objective: to identify numbers by sight and put them in the correct numerical order.
Materials needed: string, clothespins, construction paper, and a marker.

String a line from one side of the room to the other. Number the pieces of construction paper one through ten. Review with the child the appearance of each number by looking at the pages you have made. Then lay the sheets in random order on the floor. Let the child select the numbers and hang them with clothespins in the right order on the line.

PRE-READING *Flashcards*

Objective: to pick out the sound of a particular letter within a word and to differentiate between right and left.
Materials needed: scissors and the activity sheet (p. 129).

Cut out the individual pictures. Review the sound of the letter *S*. Help your child to state the word that each picture represents. Listen for the sound of *S* within the word. Does it

occur at the beginning or the end of the word? Place all the cards that begin with *S* to the child's left, all the words that end with the sound of *S* to his right. Help him to learn his right hand from his left. Reshuffle the cards and begin again, this time letting your child place the cards to his right or left.

WEEK FOUR

CHARACTER *Mother Says*

Objective: to instill a response of obedience through the reinforcement of Scripture and a repetitious game.

Learn together Ephesians 6:1. After you have the Scripture down pat, play a modified version of "Simon Says." To play the game, one person gives the other a series of instructions. (Touch your nose, wave your hand, nod your head, etc.) The only ones to be obeyed, however, are the ones that are prefaced with the words, "Mommy says"— or—"Daddy says." What really makes the game a challenge is when the leader demonstrates all of the requests. The follower is tempted to imitate and forgets to wait for the important words, "Mommy says."

OUR WORLD *Family Belongings*

Objective: to review the distinctives of each member of the family and to establish as sacred those things that cannot be shared.
Materials needed: several personal items from each member of the family that are characteristically theirs (i.e.: moms' glasses, dad's gun (unloaded), brother's model, sister's Bible, etc.).

Lay all the items on the table and floor. Look at each one and let your child identify to whom it belongs. Talk about how to treat something that is not yours. What should you do when you would like to borrow it?

What should you do when an item is off limits? How do you share with others the things that can be shared? How do you treat an item that you are borrowing? What if it gets broken?

WORD CONCEPTS *Up and Down Exploration*

Objective: to get a new view of the world while establishing the contrast between *up* and *down.*

Discover vistas never yet inspected by child's eyes. Use a ladder or step stool to look *up* . . . on top of the refrigerator, at an abandoned bird's nest in the eaves, in the rafters of the garage, or in the branches of a tree alight with autumn colors. Get down on hands and knees to look *down* . . . at an anthill alive with ants preparing for the onset of cold weather, on the bottom shelf of the pantry, under a bed, at the parts of the engine under a well-braked car. Unearth territory as yet unexplored by your child. Use the words *up* and *down* to provide reference points.

PRE-MATH *How many?*

Objective: to review the counting procedure and to associate a verbal number with a written number.

Materials needed: crayons and the activity sheet (p. 131).

Circle the appropriate number next to each symbol after counting how many of the same item can be found in the house. After the sheet is complete, talk about what a home means to a family. Discuss the many different kinds of residences there are. Talk about the places that you and your family have called home. Think about what it would be like to move somewhere else.

PRE-READING *Alphabet Tablecloth*

Objective: to give practice in the formation of many of the letters in the alphabet.

Materials needed: paper (large sheets or butcher block), masking tape, and crayons.

Cover the entire surface of your table with the paper. Tape it down so that it will not slide. Work on decorating the giant paper tablecloth with colorful crayon letters of the alphabet. At each family member's accustomed seat you could put their initials or name. Intersperse the letters with pictures of the family and things the family likes to do.

Help Balaam to make it safely back home where he belongs.

September 1

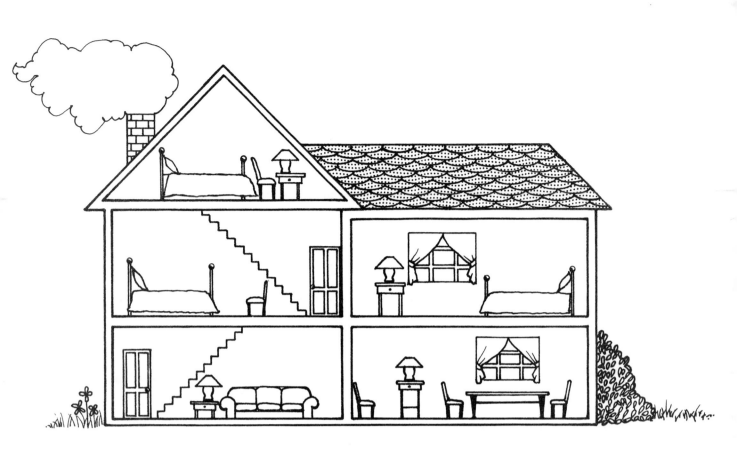

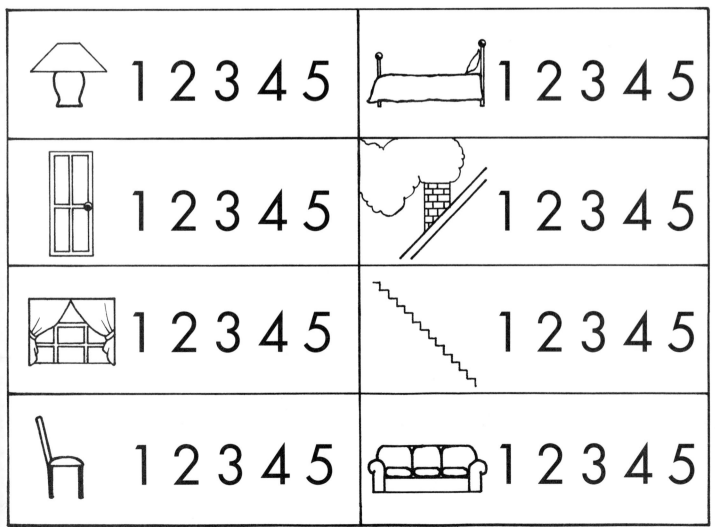

1 2 3 4 5

1 2 3 4 5

1 2 3 4 5

1 2 3 4 5

1 2 3 4 5

1 2 3 4 5

1 2 3 4 5

1 2 3 4 5

O C T O B E R

CHARACTER: honesty

OUR WORLD: animals

WORDS: wild/tame, rough/smooth, high/low

Have you ever come home to a family dog who's been patiently awaiting your arrival? The riotous movement of his tail and the abandonment of his wriggling body show you the ecstasy he feels. You alone are the object of his loving gaze and a glance into his frank and honest eyes reveals the depths of true sincerity. What you see is what you get. How appropriate that honesty and animals are the two areas of study for this month.

What a shame that when it comes to telling the truth, we are not more like the animals. They are incapable of the human hypocrisies our society endorses. Can it be that

you teach deceitfulness to your children by a lifestyle that says, "Do as I say, but don't do as I do?" A furry brown bear, a buff feathered woodcock, a web-footed otter, and a wide-winged goose are just some of many in the animal kingdom that teach their young primarily through example. They would not know how to communicate one thing and then do another. On the other hand, a passion for the truth and wholehearted integrity, even among those that name the name of Christ, is hard to find on the human level.

Take a candid look at the way you handle your own children. Have you ever glanced at

133

the face of your child and seen an expression there that you wish you could erase but you know mirrors a similar look on your own face? Has your child ever given utterance to a word or phrase you would rather him not use, but you know is repeated from your own vocabulary? Have you ever had to explain to your child why you did not speak the absolute truth in an awkward situation? The highest favor we can grant our children is our own example unencumbered by a double standard. The honesty we espouse can best be relayed in the conscientious uprightness of our own lives.

WEEK ONE

CHARACTER *King Saul Lies*

Objective: to teach that lying is never acceptable no matter who you are.

Tell the story that follows, based on 1 Samuel 15:10-26. After you are done, talk about how the animal sounds gave King Saul's lie away. Play a game by making different animal sounds and letting your child guess what animal you are imitating. Let your child make some animal noises for you.

King Saul was a great big man. Even when he was surrounded by a crowd of people, he towered head and shoulders over the others. He was good-looking and acted like a great king should.

God used King Saul and his army many times to fight against bad people. But one time, Saul did something very foolish. God had told him to completely destroy all the wicked people in battle. But Saul decided that it would be alright to keep the enemy king alive as a servant and to keep some of the nice things that the bad men owned. He set aside some of their best animals for his own.

When God saw that King Saul had disobeyed and did not destroy everything, God sent Samuel, His minister, to talk to Saul. Then Saul did something that made God even more sad. King Saul said, "Look, Samuel. I have obeyed the Lord. I killed all the bad people and saved nothing for myself." Was the king telling the truth? No!

All of a sudden, the cows began to "Moooo" and the sheep began to "Baaaah." Samuel said to Saul, "If you really did destroy all the people and everything belonging to them, what is this noise that I am hearing?" King Saul's face began to turn red. He had been caught in a lie.

In Saul's heart, he never felt sorry for what he had done, and because he didn't turn away from his sin, he never was a very great king again.

OUR WORLD *Animal Food*

Objective: to illustrate the eating habits of a variety of animals.
Materials needed: several food items.

Fix a nutritious lunch that even an animal might enjoy. For example, elephants would eat peanuts, cats would drink milk, monkeys would like bananas, and turtles would munch on celery. Combine all these food items as well as others to have a delicious meal. To make it truly authentic, eat the items as if you were actually the animal.

WORD CONCEPTS *Rope Jumping*

Objective: to see a visual demonstration of *high* versus *low*.
Materials needed: a rope.

Tie one end of the rope to a post (or table leg or whatever) and hold the other end off the ground. Let your child see how high he can jump, given a running start. Make verbal reference to whether the rope is *low* or *high* as you raise it for each successive jump. Next, see if the child can squeeze under the rope by bending backward. Bring it lower after each try.

PRE-MATH *Number Mosaic*

Objective: to reiterate how the number three is formed.

Materials needed: several colors of construction paper cut into many tiny squares, glue, and a large piece of construction paper.

Using the large piece of construction paper as a background, assist the child in sketching a number three in pencil. With this as a guide, apply the tiny squares onto the outline with the glue. Set them side by side to give the appearance of a whole motif done in tile.

PRE-READING *Back Tracing*

Objective: to remember how to make some of the letters of the alphabet.

Lift up your child's shirt and trace a letter on his back to see if he can identify it. Have him trace some letters on your back. Stick to simpler, nonreversible letters when you are the one doing the drawing.

W E E K   T W O

CHARACTER *The Cookie Lie*

Objective: to understand that honesty brings reward and lying brings consequence.

Materials needed: cookies and milk.

Tell the following story in such a way that your child feels involved. Build to a grand climax. What should the character do? End the story with a cookie and a glass of milk. Talk the story over as you partake of this visual illustration.

Chocolate chip cookies! Sammy loved the smell. "Oh, Mom!" he cried. "Can I have one?" He reached up to the counter where the cookies were laid out to cool.

"You will have to wait till later. I don't want you to spoil your supper," she said smiling at his enthusiasm. Then she left the room to set the table for dinner. Sammy was so disappointed. His mom had no idea how hard he had played all afternoon and how hungry he really was. There was no way he could wait.

Maybe he could try a tiny bite on the side of one. But hardly before he realized what was happening, the whole cookie kind of slid all the way down his throat into his tummy. Mmmm. It was great! But now as he looked at the neat rows where all the cookies were laid out, he realized that there was a spot that was obviously bare. He'd have to eat another one to even out the rows. In no time, he had downed five cookies and now all the rows were even.

"Supper time!" Mom called. Ughhh. Sammy wasn't a bit hungry any more.

As everyone sat down to the table, Dad made an announcement. "I think that we should treat everyone who eats a good dinner tonight to a special trip to the ice cream shop. How about it?" Sammy's brothers and sisters cheered while Sammy groaned. Normally he would have loved ice cream, but right now all those cookies in his tummy weren't making him feel very good.

"What's wrong?" his mother asked. "Aren't you hungry? You didn't have anything to eat before dinner did you?"

"No," Sammy lied. His mother was looking right into his eyes. She looked very sad.

Then Sammy knew that he should have told the truth. A big tear ran down his cheek. "I told a whopper, Mom," he confessed. "I ate some of your cookies."

"I know," she said. "I saw the crumbs on your face. But now I'm afraid you're going to miss a good dinner and a fun family outing. Would you like to go and lie down?" Sammy nodded.

OUR WORLD *Borrowing a Pet*

Objective: to learn the responsibility of animal care.

Materials needed: a borrowed pet. Suggestion: a gerbil, goldfish, turtle, iguana, bunny, or puppy.

Select the pet of a friend to baby-sit for a few days. Choose one that will not be affected by a change in environment. Teach your child proper animal care. For example, show your child how much food to sprinkle in a fish bowl or how to gently hold a gerbil. Is the animal wild or tame? Your child will be too young to take full responsibility, but he can do a lot to assist in the animal's maintenance. He can help wash out a cage, change water, or replace food, all under your supervision.

WORD CONCEPTS *Animal Mural*

Objective: to notice some of the differences between *wild* and *tame* animals.
Materials needed: large sheet of paper, magazines, glue, and crayons.

Look through the magazines and tear out animal and bird pictures. Attach a large sheet of paper to the wall, making it accessible to your child. Draw homes for the animals that have been selected (nests for birds, corrals for horses, caves for bears, houses for dogs, etc.) Tie it all together with land, trees, skies, and seas. Apply glue to the back of the magazine pictures that you have picked and place them where they belong in the scene. Differentiate between *wild* and *tame* animals. Do they live in the same kinds of places? Are their needs met in the same way?

PRE-MATH *Animals in Camouflage*

Objective: to learn to count objects only once when numbering.
Materials needed: crayons and the activity sheet (p. 139).

Explore the picture together, looking for the ten hidden animals. Make a mark on each one as you count to be sure you only number it once. Talk about how God has provided many animals with certain colors or textures

so they blend in with their surrounding environments. Which animals have *rough* skin and which have *smooth*? Color each of the animals you have discovered in the picture. Would you ever find a purple elephant or a blue monkey?

PRE-READING *Safari Hunt*

Objective: to encourage verbal expression of thought and creativity in descriptive phrases and complete sentences.

Let your imaginations run wild. Put away your inhibitions. Make preparations for a safari hunt. Mentally turn your house into an African grassland. Pretend that inanimate objects have come alive. A bed can become an elephant. Turn a chair into a lion. Ask questions to stimulate your child's story telling instincts. What kind of trouble do you think we'll find? Where shall we go? What shall we do when we get there? What was that noise? Do you see what I see? What do you think is around that corner?

WEEK THREE

CHARACTER *Two Kinds of Lies*

Objective: to point out that you can lie by omission and commission.

Tell the following imaginary story. Perhaps you can find a special corner, window seat, or part of a bed that is your unique place for storytelling. Whenever you resort to that particular spot, your child can be primed for a wonderful tale and ready to listen.

Far off in outer space, there was a planet named *Snarf*. It was always covered with a thick blanket of snow, which is why the little robot creatures that tunneled and plowed hundreds of passageways under the surface were called *Snobots*.

The littlest Snobot on the whole planet of Snarf was named Crick. Right now he was bouncing up and down on his springs with excitement. His teacher at school was announcing a romp on Snowglen Mountain and all the junior Snobots were invited.

The day of the romp arrived and Crick was at the school grounds early. After all the Snobots arrived, they would tunnel their way to the mountain for a jolly time of recreation. All of a sudden, Crick panicked. The teacher had told them to bring plenty of lubricating oil as mechanical joints have a tendency to stick in the cold. Crick had carefully placed his little can in the drawer in his body just under his right arm, but now it was gone. He did not have any time to go back home and get another one either.

The teacher was asking some questions. "Are all the Snobots ready to go? Has everyone brought their can of lubricating oil?" Crick did not say anything. He did not want to miss out on the trip.

It was a wonderful hike. Crick scooted and bounced around all of the others as they made their way quickly down the mountain. All of a sudden, before he could say a word, Crick felt his joints and wheels freeze tight. And not a drop of oil on hand. All of the others were hurrying on ahead and getting farther away in the distance. Would he be left to rust in the snow forever? Oh, if only he had told his teacher that he had lost his oil when she asked.

Just then, he felt a trickle of oil on his back wheel and under his front spring. Then his teacher came into view and loosened his frozen jaw. "I always follow behind in case there are any stragglers," she said. Crick was so relieved he almost cried.

"I lost my oil," he confessed. "But I wanted to go on the romp so badly that I didn't want to tell you."

"You know," said his teacher softly. "I think you have learned today that there are two kinds of lies. One is when you say something that is not true. Another is when you say nothing at all, so that someone thinks something that is not true. Both are just as dangerous. Come on now. Let's catch up with the rest."

OUR WORLD Animals in Our Lives

Objective: to emphasize the role that animals play in our lives.
Materials needed: various animal-related food and clothing items.

Scan your pantry and refrigerator shelves for all the food that you have on hand that has been contributed by animals. Check your closets and linen cupboards for leather and wool products. The quantity of items you congregate will emphasize the vital part that animals play in our lives. Assist your child in naming the animal each item comes from. Did the animal have to give its life in order for people to benefit?

WORD CONCEPTS Paper Airplane

Objective: to distinguish between *high* and *low*.
Materials needed: paper.

Fold some paper airplanes. Experiment with different styles. Have a contest to see whose plane will go the farthest, stay the longest in the air, and perform tricks. Ask your child to evaluate whether he thinks each flight was *high* or *low*.

PRE-MATH Leapfrog

Objective: to provide another source for counting that is related to the animal theme.

Measure your backyard and/or living room by leapfrogs. How many does it take to go from one side to another? To leapfrog, one person must squat with his head on the ground while the other vaults over his back and lands a little beyond. Wherever the second person lands, it is his turn to crouch while the original person uses the newly available back as a springboard to leap ahead. Cross the distance to be measured, counting each jump.

PRE-READING *Barnyard Animals*

Objective: to hear the beginning sound of a word and to correlate it with a written letter.
Materials needed: scissors, glue, and the activity page (p. 141).

Let your child cut out each animal figure square as he verbalizes the sound that starts its name. Look for the corresponding letter in the barnyard to know where each animal is to be placed. Glue it in the appropriate spot. Are farm animals *wild* or *tame?*

WEEK FOUR

CHARACTER *Honesty Game*

Objective: to set up real life applications of honesty and to drive home the truth that "your sin will find you out" (Num. 32:23).
Materials needed: token for each person (paper clip, button, etc.), a coin, and the game board (p. 143).

Play the game with verbal reminders that every act of dishonesty has its consequences. Include lots of laughs and hugs. Make sure that when your child lands on a square that indicates a bad choice, he knows that the game is pretend.

OUR WORLD *Animal Masks*

Objective: to encourage the child to step into the role of an animal, thus allowing him to experience what its life might be like.
Materials needed: large paper bag, scissors, glue, construction paper, markers, and cellophane tape.

Before beginning the craft, have your child put the paper bag over his head to determine where the two eye holes should be placed.

Let your child cut them out and draw the animal face. Add construction paper fur and facial features as desired. While working on the project, discuss the differences between animals and human beings. After the bag is done, let your child don the mask and assume the animal role.

WORD CONCEPTS *Carpentry*

Objective: to see and feel the difference between *rough* and *smooth.*
Materials needed: sandpaper and an unfinished wooden board.

Feel the texture of the wood. Is it *rough* or *smooth?* Let your child apply the sandpaper, rubbing and checking periodically for a difference in the feel. Praise and admire his hard work when the wood is finally made smooth.

PRE-MATH *Counting Legs*

Objective: to associate various objects that relate to the same number.

Ask your child to count everything around the house that has four legs (tables, dressers, chairs, couches, cats, etc.). Your child might need some prompting if he is a slow starter. Tell him when he is close to something that might fit into this category.

PRE-READING *Letter Pancakes*

Objective: to allow for letter identification in an unusual medium.
Materials needed: pancake batter and a hot griddle.

Take a teaspoon and drizzle the batter onto the griddle in the shape of a letter (perhaps the child's initials). Remember to invert the letters as they will appear like a mirrored image. Pour batter over each letter shape. Let the child name the letters and the sounds they make as each pancake is served.

Find the ten hidden animals, then color the picture.

October 1

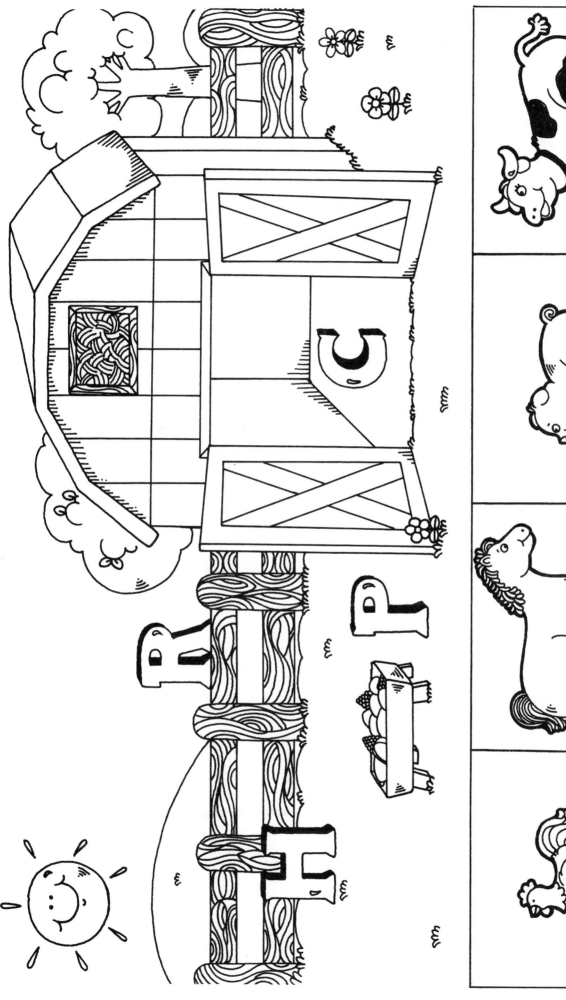

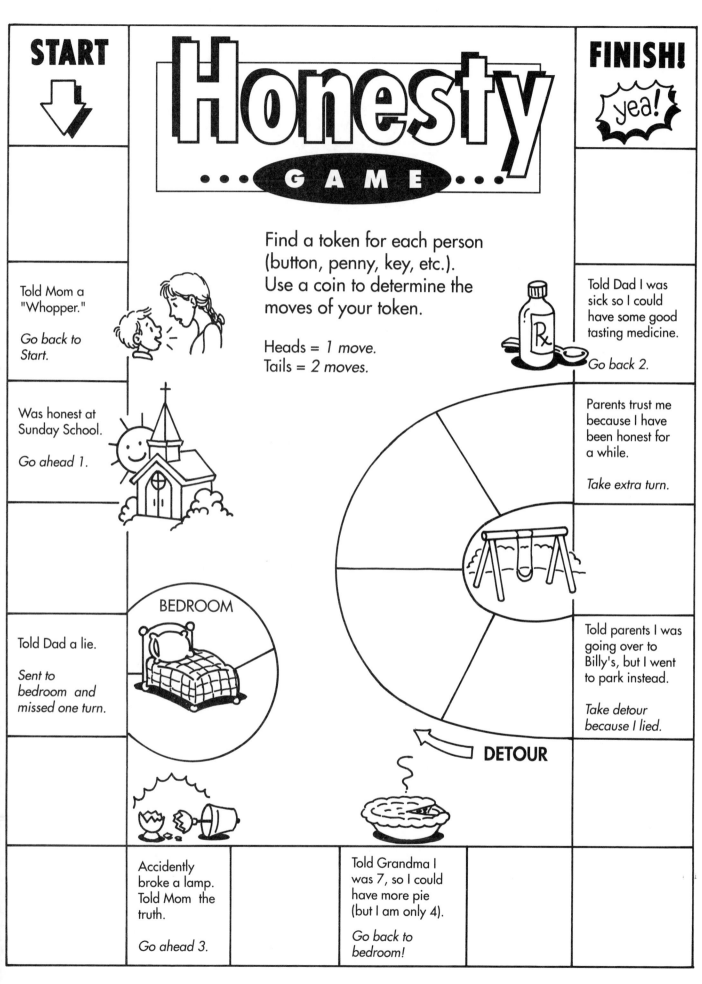

START

Honesty ....G A M E....

FINISH! yea!

Find a token for each person (button, penny, key, etc.). Use a coin to determine the moves of your token.

Heads = *1 move.*
Tails = *2 moves.*

Told Mom a "Whopper."
Go back to Start.

Was honest at Sunday School.
Go ahead 1.

Told Dad I was sick so I could have some good tasting medicine.
Go back 2.

Parents trust me because I have been honest for a while.
Take extra turn.

BEDROOM

Told Dad a lie.
Sent to bedroom and missed one turn.

Told parents I was going over to Billy's, but I went to park instead.
Take detour because I lied.

DETOUR

Accidently broke a lamp. Told Mom the truth.
Go ahead 3.

Told Grandma I was 7, so I could have more pie (but I am only 4).
Go back to bedroom!

October 3

N O V E M B E R

CHARACTER: thankfulness
OUR WORLD: world customs
WORDS: close/far, soft/hard, behind/before

Can't you just imagine watching narrow bamboo poles being struck rhythmically together during a dance on a South Pacific island? Or smelling the bakery fresh aroma of long baguette loaves to be eaten for breakfast in Paris, France? Or viewing the huge form of an elephant, decoratively painted, shuffling along an autumn festival parade in India? Or hearing the clack of wooden shoes on cobblestone streets in Holland? Or trying to catch a smile on the face of a uniformed guard at Buckingham Palace in England? Or hearing the sambas echoing through the streets of Brasilia, Brazil the week before

Easter? How wonderful if we could grasp samplings like these from all around the world to enrich our lives.

This month, we'll display for our children a fascinating variety of customs from as many cultures as we can. At the same time, we will introduce the character quality of thankfulness. In this way, we can present a favorite tradition from our own country— Thanksgiving Day. "Lord, help us to set aside our pampered American contempt. Help us to catch a spirit of genuine appreciation for all the things we have from other people around the world. Help us to teach our children that giving thanks is an attitude of the heart to be celebrated every day.''

How encouraging to know that according to Psalm 139, there is nowhere on planet earth that we could visit where God is not already present. His care does not change with location, and the fellowship of believers is worldwide. If we listen very carefully, I believe we can catch whispers of gratitude in many languages from around the world that might transform our own tendency to be spoiled. Arigato (Japanese), Gracias (Spanish), Takk (Hebrew), Merci (French), Danke schön (German). Thank you, God!

WEEK ONE

CHARACTER *Memory Stones*

Objective: to create a visual reminder of God's blessings and our gratitude.
Materials needed: twelve stones.

Tell the following story, originating from Joshua 3:14-4:9. Think with your child of times in his life when God has done something special. In memory of these, make a pile of stones. Every time you view them, make it a point to thank God for His help and care. Whenever your child feels like he wants to complain, take a new look at the rocks.

God's people were almost to the new land that God had promised them. As a matter of fact, only one thing stood between them and the home for which they had been waiting so long. That was the mighty Jordan River. It was wide and deep. Would they ever get across?

But God, who had brought them safely this far, was certainly not going to let them down now. Joshua, the new leader, listened carefully as God instructed him. The priests (ministers of God), should walk into the river carrying the Ark (a special golden box full of

keepsakes). All the people should pick up their belongings and follow them.

As the feet of the priests touched the water, the river immediately stopped running. It piled up in a high wall and left miles of dry ground for the people to walk over. The priests stood with the ark right in the middle of the river bed. And not one person got even the tiniest bit wet crossing to the other side.

Before the priests walked out of the place where the river normally flowed, Joshua had the people stack twelve large stones in the middle. There was one for each of the family groups. Then he called the priests out of the Jordan. As soon as their feet touched the shore, the river rushed into its place with a mighty roar once again. But the tower of rocks could still be seen jutting up from the mass of churning water.

Joshua told the people that the tower would help them and their children recall that God was their helper. They could use that marker as a reminder to be thankful to the God who is mightier than all the earth.

OUR WORLD *Shoji Screen*

Objective: to see beauty in other cultures of the world.
Materials needed: wax paper, liquid starch, brush, yarn, and bits of nature (flower petals, leaves, pine needles, grass, etc.).

Help your child cut a square of waxed paper and then brush on a layer of starch. With this as a background, let him arrange his pieces from nature however his artistic instincts suggest. Place another piece of waxed paper over this arrangement. Gently press with your fingers. After it has dried, punch holes in the top and hang it in the window with yarn. Enjoy the lovely design. Talk about how an oriental home would differ from ours by using these translucent screens to divide one room from another. Think of eating with chopsticks at low tables while sitting on pillows. Imagine what it would be like to roll up the mat you sleep on and place it out of the way for the day.

WORD CONCEPTS *Wall Shadows*

Objectives: to demonstrate the meaning of *behind* and *before* through the use of shadows.

Set up a bright light in a dark room for some shadow play. Demonstrate for your child how to pose hands and body to make pictures on the wall. Note particularly what happens when one individual stands, between the first person and the light. Use the words *behind* and *before* to describe what is happening.

PRE-MATH *Dice Challenge*

Objective: to associate a verbal number with a visual number of objects.
Materials needed: dice.

The object of the game is to be the first to completely hop around the room. You must take turns and only hop the number of times the die indicates. Count the number of dots, state the number, then count out the appropriate number of jumps.

PRE-READING *Upper and Lower Case Letters*

Objective: to see that there are two ways of writing one letter.
Materials needed: index cards, markers, and a stapler.

Choose a number of alphabetical letters to study. Write the capital letter on one card and the lower case on another. Review the letters like flashcards. Then shuffle the cards, and let your child match the letters that belong together. Once he finds a match, help him to use a stapler to fasten them together.

WEEK TWO

CHARACTER *Psalm 95:2*

Objective: to memorize a verse and make immediate application.
Materials needed: a comb and waxed paper.

Work together on implanting the following verse in your hearts: "Come before God with thanksgiving, and praise Him with music and song" (author's paraphrase).

After the words have become familiar, make a kazoo type instrument by folding a piece of waxed paper over the teeth of a comb. Place it lightly in your mouth and hum. The vibrations will make an unusual sounding instrument for you to make your praise music to God.

OUR WORLD *Tortillas*

Objective: to realize all the different ways that food can be prepared around the world.
Materials needed: 1 cup flour, 1 Tbs. shortening, 1/2 tsp. salt, 1/2 tsp. baking powder, 1/3 cup warm milk, a mixing bowl, and a skillet.

Mix together the first four ingredients. Slowly stir in the warm milk. Knead on a floured surface. Roll out six flat circles. Cook in an ungreased skillet over medium heat. Eat plain, buttered, or with a filling. Talk about all the foods your child enjoys that have their origins in another country. Describe some exotic meals that your child may never have tasted. Talk about different but wonderful food around the world.

WORD CONCEPTS *Paperwork*

Objective: to teach the child to follow instructions related to the concept words of the month.
Materials needed: crayons and the activity sheet (p. 153).

Look at the picture and give the following instructions:

(1) Draw a circle around something that is far away.

(2) Put an X on someone that is near.

(3) Underline something that is soft.

(4) Put a square around something that is hard.

(5) Color someone that is behind the table.

(6) Outline someone that is before the table.

Explain to your child what the direction is asking him to do. After he has done what is asked, color the picture together while talking about what the first Thanksgiving was like and how you will be celebrating your holiday this year.

PRE-MATH *Hopscotch*

Objective: to see a numeral and know what it is.
Materials needed: chalk.

With the chalk, draw a series of large blocks on your sidewalk, patio, or garage floor to form a hopscotch game. Number each of the squares. Try to jump in each block with one foot, hopping to the end of the boxes and back. You must call out the number of each square that you land in. If you miss the square, or step on a line, your turn passes on to another person.

PRE-READING *Cotton Ball Letters*

Objective: to practice forming some alphabetical letters and to experience the feeling of *hard* and *soft*.
Materials needed: plywood or cardboard, cotton balls, a pencil, and glue.

Touch and feel the contrast between the *hard* surface of the wood or cardboard and the fluffy *softness* of the cotton. Let your child outline several letters (try to pick some that are unfamiliar and need practice) on the background of wood or cardboard. Dab the cotton balls with glue and place on the lines to form letters out of the cotton.

W E E K   T H R E E

CHARACTER *Woman with Spices*

Objective: to show that a heart full of gratitude needs to be expressed.

Materials needed: perfumes, colognes, or other sweet smelling substances.

Assemble a variety of pleasant aromas to be sampled and smelled before the story. Tell the following narrative about the woman who had such a thankful heart that she gave away the most valuable thing she could think of—perfume (Mark 14:3-9; John 12:1-8). After the story, talk about how a thankful spirit needs to be expressed. Is there somebody that your child might call and speak to on the phone that deserves a word of thanks?

When Jesus was alive on the earth, He spent His time doing good things for other people. Many sick and hurt people were healed by a touch from His hand or a word from His lips. Simon the leper was completely cured of a terrible disease when He believed that Jesus would heal him. He was thankful for what Jesus had done and loved Him with all of his heart. So he invited Jesus and His helpers to celebrate one of the holidays at his house. Many people showed up for the party and when it was time to eat they all gathered around the table.

But healing the sick was not the only good thing that Jesus did when He was here on earth. He also took care of the hurt that comes inside of people. He took away the sins that kept people from knowing God. A woman named Mary was one of those people to whom Jesus said, "Your sins are forgiven." And just like Simon, she loved Jesus and wanted to find some way to say "thank you" to Him.

But what could she do? She thought and thought. Finally, she decided on the perfect thing. She would buy Jesus a bottle of very expensive perfume. Its delicious smell would tell Him of her appreciation. She went through all her purses, drawers, and boxes looking for every last penny she owned. At last she had enough. She would have to hurry to buy the perfume and give it to Jesus while He was still in town.

It was just as Jesus was sitting down to eat at Simon's house that Mary burst breathlessly through the door with her gift. Without a word she carefully poured some of the costly perfume on His head and His feet. With great tenderness and love, she wiped His feet with her long hair. Would He understand her gratitude even though she could not find the words to say what was in her heart?

Some of the people watching started to grumble and put her down. They said she ought to have given the money to help the needy people instead of buying the perfume and letting it drip all over Jesus onto the floor.

But Jesus understood what was in her heart. He knew how thankful she was for what He had done. "Let her alone," He said. "You can help the poor any time you like. But I will not always be here. Mary has done a good deed. In years to come, when people talk about Me, they will always remember what Mary has done here today."

What Jesus said was true. Today, 2,000 years later, we are still telling the story about Mary and her thankful heart.

OUR WORLD   *Marshmallow Igloo*

Objective: to introduce the idea that different countries have different climates and to show how their individual cultures have adapted to them.
Materials needed: marshmallows and toothpicks.

Stick the marshmallows together with the toothpicks to form an imaginary igloo. Describe what a real Eskimo house might look like with its blocks of ice and rounded shape. Would it make a very comfortable home? Describe other types of climate in other parts of the world . . . tropical rain forests in parts of South America and Africa, arid deserts in the Middle East, four seasons in North America, etc. How would the weather make a difference in the way people live?

WORD CONCEPTS   *Musical Chair*

Objective: to illustrate in the physical realm the antonyms, *near* and *far*.

Materials needed: a chair and a radio or tape player with a music tape.

Place the chair on one side of the room. Instruct your child that as long as the music continues, he must keep moving in a set path from the chair to the opposite wall and back. When the music stops, he must freeze right where he is. The parent can be in charge of turning the music on and off. The point of the game is for your child to be as near to the chair as possible when the music stops playing. Use this game as an opportunity to present the words *near* and *far*, and to use them as often as possible.

PRE-MATH   *Bobbing for Apples*

Objective: to teach numbers and simple addition principles.
Materials needed: a large tub of water, six to ten apples, and a knife.

Notch each of the apples with a different number of marks. These will indicate how many points are to be scored when each apple is caught with your teeth. Put the apples in the tub of water and take turns bobbing for them until all of them have been snagged. Add up the scores to see who wins. Enjoy an apple together, counting each bite.

PRE-READING   *Alphabet Dominoes*

Objective: to be able to recognize and pair together matching letters of the alphabet.
Materials needed: scissors and the activity sheet (p. 155).

Cut the individual dominoes apart. Put them all face down, shuffle, and let each player pick five. The remaining cards should be set aside until one of the players finds he must draw. Any person with a double letter card may begin by placing his card face up on the table. The next person must match one of the letters on the card with a card of his own or draw until he finds one to match. A player may match any letter that has not already been played on. The object is to be the first to run out of cards.

WEEK FOUR

CHARACTER *Tic-Tac-Toe*

Objective: to force the child to think beyond rudimentary replies about all the things for which he is grateful.
Materials needed: paper and pencil.

Teach your child to play tic-tac-toe. Draw two parallel horizontal and two parallel vertical lines running through each other on the paper. Use this as the basis for the game which requires each player to try to get three of his own marks in a row. One player can draw *X's* and the other player can draw *Os*. Each player must take turns deciding which square to claim as his own. Add another dimension to the game by requiring each player to state something for which he is thankful before he can make his move.

OUR WORLD *Costumes of Other Lands*

Objective: to see that there are many attractive and practical ways to dress all over the world.
Materials needed: crayons and the activity sheet (p. 157).

Help your child to match the clothes and the children on the sheet. Talk about the lands from which they came. Are there reasons for which a person might choose one costume over another? Enlarge the discussion by asking your child to state differences and similarities between himself and any other children on the page. How about in the eyes of God? Does He view us differently?

WORD CONCEPTS *Museum Display*

Objective: to let your child develop his own powers of analysis by distinguishing between *soft* and *hard*.
Materials needed: two medium-sized boxes.

Let your child take first one box and then the other, perusing the house for items to assemble. The first box can be filled with things that are *soft*. The second can hold representatives for *hard*. Let your child act as a museum curator in presenting to you the collectibles he has found. Let him state the name of the item, where it was found, and the category to which it belongs.

PRE-MATH *Going to Market*

Objective: to enhance counting skills by giving an opportunity to handle money.
Materials needed: canned and boxed goods, grocery bags, index cards, markers, and pennies.

Play store. You can set up a mock supermarket by displaying various grocery items on a shelf. Use the index cards to state simplified prices . . . two cents for a can of beans, seven cents for a box of baking soda, etc. Let your child make his selections, count out enough pennies for each item, and take his bagged purchases with him.

PRE-READING *Letter Sounds*

Objective: to help the child to become aware of the sound of *M* and to hear it within a variety of words.

Read the following story very slowly, emphasizing the sound of the letter *M*. Have the child jump to his feet whenever he hears a word that involves that letter. Read the story several times, giving a different instruction to be followed at the sound of *M* each time you read. Perhaps your child can clap or flap his arms. Put less personal emphasis on the letter each time you read allowing the child to distinguish the sound using his own prowess instead of relying on inflection indicators in your voice.

Millions of moths flew up the mountainside to munch on some moss. It just melted in their mouths. But within minutes they realized their monstrous mistake. The music of many maddened mosquitoes was filling the air. The message of the mosquitoes was meaningful. The moss was their meal. The mosquitoes would make those meddlesome moths miserable. They mobbed them mercilessly. The moths mourned. Have you ever seen a moth bawl?

November 1

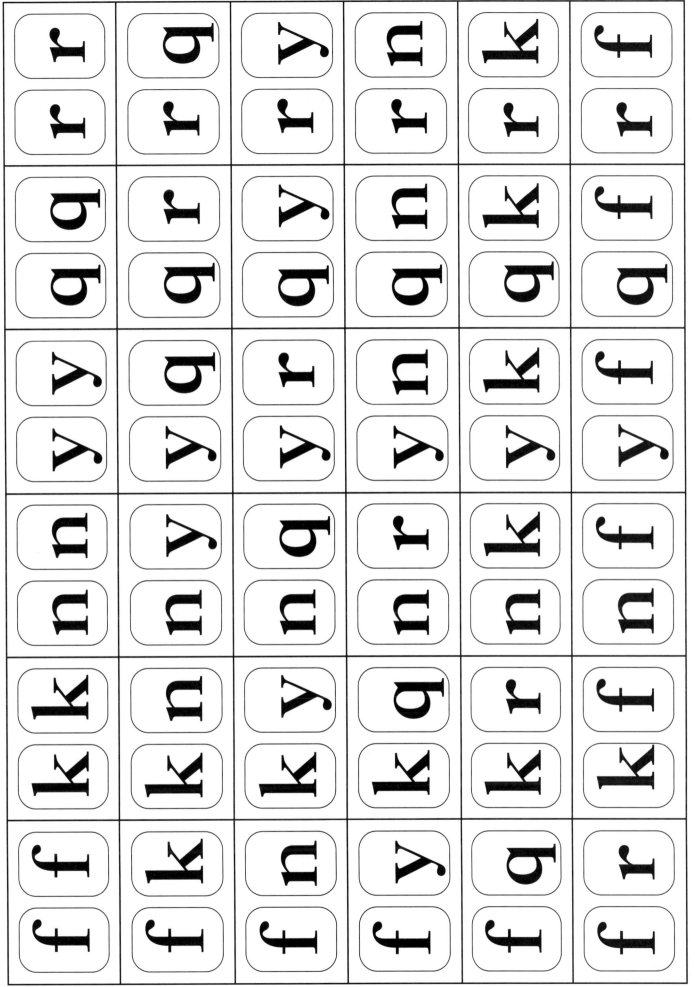

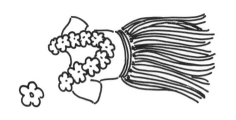 

HAWAII

 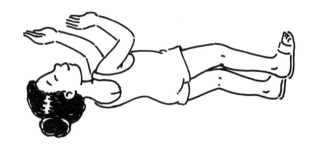

CHINA

 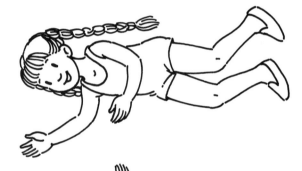

NORWAY

BRAZIL

 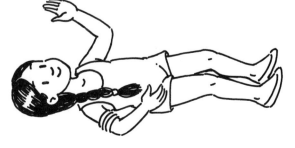

INDIA

D E C E M B E R

| CHARACTER: giving |
| OUR WORLD: weather and seasons |
| WORDS: in/out, hot/cold, heavy/light |

What a blustery and tempestuous month to be talking about the weather. As the fury of winter storms commence their seasonal raging, my natural tendency is to draw into my self. Give me a comfortable chair, a good book, and a loving family around a roaring hearth and I'm in blissful happiness. I could easily shut the windows and doors against the rest of the world and as long as I had a full pantry and a few meaningful projects, I would not open them again until spring.

Fortunately, to save me from myself, the Christmas season always intervenes. How I need this holiday, flung deliberately into the middle of the time that bears and squirrels would suggest I hibernate. The very point of the day is to forget my own ease and comfort, reaching out to bless others instead. That is certainly the example set by our Lord. Philippians 2:6-7 tells of the glories He left behind to pour Himself out for the world. First, He came as a baby. Later, He died as a man. Hopefully, as we study the character quality of giving, it will become a natural response in our lives as well as the lives of our children.

I am reminded of Tabitha in the New Testament, who flooded the poor with thoughtful gifts that she had made herself. When she died, a crowd of people squeezed into her house, weeping and holding up all that she had labored over and given away. The people loved her for her considerate and sacrificial heart.

When I die, I don't want people to say, "So what?!" But like Tabitha, I want my life to count. Can you raise your children with that same sense of purpose? Will you save them from the mentality that says, "I demand to be served and entertained"? If so, you will have to be the one to extend yourself in reaching out to a needy world. You will have to retrain your natural impulse toward an inward focus. You will have to show them how to share with others what they are and have.

WEEK ONE

CHARACTER *A Little Boy's Lunch*

Objective: to show that God can do big things with even the little that I have, if only I'm willing to give.

Materials needed: a pencil and the activity sheet (p. 167).

Tell the following story, taken from John 6:5-13. Review it together afterward by working on the activity sheet. Compare the small numbers that represent the original lunch with the large number of people it fed and the amount left over. God made little into much!

A little boy ran up to his mother. He was so excited he could scarcely talk. As he caught his breath, he blurted out the news that Jesus was coming! He had heard that wherever Jesus went, wonderful things would happen. He wanted to see them for himself. Would his mother let him go?

His mother smiled at the boy's enthusiasm. She would let him see Jesus. But first

the boy must pack a little something to eat in case he didn't make it back in time for lunch. They wrapped five rolls of bread and two little fish to stow in a basket. "Thanks Mom," he called over his shoulder as he ran out to join the crowds of people who were hurrying down the main road. Everyone wanted to hear Jesus preach and watch Him heal the sick.

Jesus was speaking on a grassy mountain slope. When the boy arrived, many people were sitting around listening intently. The boy moved up as close as he dared and sprawled on a clump of grass to catch whatever words he could. Time passed quickly, for the stories that Jesus told held the boy's interest. He could have listened for hours.

Soon it grew late and everyone began to realize that it was past suppertime. No one had thought to bring any food except the little boy. He could hear the friends of Jesus worrying among themselves that there was no place to buy food for all the people, and besides, they had no money anyway. It only took the boy a minute to decide what he wanted to do. After listening to the words of Jesus, the boy knew that he loved Him. He would give his lunch to Jesus.

Holding out his basket, he walked right up to Jesus. The people around him laughed. "Does he really think such a little lunch could possibly feed all these people?" they asked.

But Jesus did not laugh. He had everyone sit down and then He bowed His head and thanked God for providing the food. Watching in amazement, the boy saw Jesus pick up the five rolls he had packed just that morning and break them into enough pieces that everyone would be able to have some. Jesus' helpers hurried to give the food away. The bread and the fish never ran out until all the people had been served! All the people ate until they were completely full.

As a matter of fact, there was so much, that twelve baskets full of food were left over. All because a little boy had been willing to share what he had.

OUR WORLD *Weather Gauge*

Objective: to become aware of weather patterns and predominate seasonal trends.
Materials needed: paper plate, ruler, markers, brad, scissors, and construction paper.

Using the ruler, draw pie-shaped wedges on the paper plate. Depict a different weather condition within each division: cloudy, sunny, rainy, snowy, foggy, windy, etc. Cut an arrow out of the construction paper and fasten with a brad to the center of the plate. Turn the arrow to indicate the present status of weather.

WORD CONCEPTS *Warm Water*

Objective: to demonstrate how temperature can be altered to feel the sensation of *hot* and *cold.*
Materials needed: four containers: one empty, one with hot water, one with warm water, and one with cold water.

Let your child feel the differences between the water temperature in each of the containers. Let him mix the water from the hot and cold containers into the empty one until he establishes a perfect match with the water in the warm container. Talk about when you would want hot water (for cooking, cleaning), cold water (for swimming, drinking), and warm water (for bathing). What was happening when you mixed the *cold* water with the *hot?*

PRE-MATH *Countdown*

Objective: to count something that is of primary interest to the child.
Materials needed: a calendar and a pencil.

Count how many days are left until Christmas. Use the calendar as a reference and make a small mark with the pencil on each day that you count. Study the calendar to discover other interesting facts, such as how many months are in a year, when other holidays occur, approximate days in a month, etc.

PRE-READING *Yes and No*

Objective: to teach the spelling of the words *yes* and *no* by recognition and response.
Materials needed: two sheets of construction paper and a marker.

Print *YES* on one sheet and *NO* on the other. Have your child hold one of these papers in each hand. Ask questions that require a yes or no answer. You might ask, "Do you like to throw snowballs?"—or—"Have you wrapped any Christmas presents?"—or—"Are any daffodils blooming in the yard?" Let your child respond by raising the appropriate card. During the course of the game, look closely together at the spelling of each word. Reverse the cards occasionally, forcing your child to study the words and not the order.

WEEK TWO

CHARACTER *Bulgy Bear*

Objective: to stress the attitude of giving over the value of the gift.
Materials needed: 1 cup oatmeal, $\frac{1}{3}$ cup wheat germ, $\frac{1}{4}$ cup coconut, $\frac{1}{4}$ cup chopped nuts, $\frac{1}{4}$ cup powdered milk, 1 tsp. cinnamon, 2 Tbs. honey, 2 Tbs. oil, 1 tsp. vanilla, a bowl, a cookie sheet, and paper towels.

After relating the following story in which nuts and honey play a predominant part, make a batch of granola that includes both of these items. Mix the first six ingredients together. Add the rest and mix again. Spread on a cookie sheet. Bake at 375 degrees for 8 to 10 minutes. Cool the granola on paper towels and eat as a snack or cereal.

Once upon a time, there was a little squirrel named Squeaky. He had a very good friend named Bulgy. His friend was a bear. It was Bulgy's birthday and Squeaky knew exactly what he was going to give him. From a secret drawer where the squirrel had been saving them for months, he took out a small package of nuts. Wouldn't Bulgy be surprised! Nuts were Squeaky's favorite treat, and he was sure that Bulgy would love them too.

After he finished tying a bow around the present, Squeaky started down the trail to Bulgy's house. But as he scurried along, he met Sam. Sam was a loudmouthed bluejay, and he had his eye cocked on the gift in Squeaky's hand. It was just the right size and shape. Could it be walnuts? "Why, hello, my good buddy, my pal," Sam began. "How nice of you to think of me on this bright, crisp day. I was just wondering how a delicious, crunchy walnut would taste in my poor, empty tummy. And here you came with a package just for me."

Before Squeaky had a chance to blurt out even one word, the bird snatched the gift out of his paw, pried open the shells, and popped the nutmeats into his mouth. The empty hulls clattered on the ground.

With tears in his eyes, Squeaky stuck the discarded shells into his pocket. He felt awful because now he had nothing to give his friend. How could he wish him a happy birthday? He had been so proud to present Bulgy with those nuts. He started to run down the path toward Bulgy's house. But he should have been watching where he was going. He was crying so hard that he ran headlong into an old beehive. Now he was covered head to foot with sticky-icky honey. By the time he finally got to Bulgy's house, he was a terrible mess. Between sobs, he tried to tell Bulgy all that had happened.

Sadly, he pulled the walnut shells out of his gummy pocket. Even they were full of honey. When he saw the shells Bulgy's eyes lit up. "Squeaky!" he exclaimed. "You have brought me little honey cups instead. It's the best present you ever could have given."

With a smile showing through his matted fur, Squeaky realized an important fact. Because he had wanted to give his best, he did.

OUR WORLD *Snow Flurry*

Objective: to learn about another weather condition and the season to which it belongs.
Materials needed: white paper, scissors, water, and a glass jar with a lid.

Cut the paper into tiny squares. Drop them into a jar filled almost to the top with water. Shut tightly with a lid, then wait until the papers have all settled to the bottom. Let the child gently shake the jar to create a snowstorm in miniature. Talk about what conditions need to be present for real snow to fall. Refer to the four seasons to decide what time of the year snow is most likely to happen.

WORD CONCEPTS *Present Wrapping*

Objective: to provide a forum for discussion of the words *in* and *out*.
Materials needed: a present, a box, paper, scissors, ribbon, and tape.

As you handle the present, ask your child to state whether it is in the box or out of the box. Continue to wrap the gift together, asking whether the box is in or out of the paper. Embellish with a ribbon and talk about whether the ribbon is *in* or *out*. Discuss the joy of giving.

PRE-MATH *Car Race*

Objective: to provide a chance to write, hear, and state several numbers.
Materials needed: four toy vehicles, paper, scissors, markers, and tape.

Write four numbers on the paper that can be cut out and taped on each car. This will prepare them for identification in the race. The child can man two of the vehicles and the parent the remaining two. Race them across a long stretch of floor to see whose will go the fastest and farthest. Call them by their numbered names. For example, "Number two went the farthest, but number fourteen seemed to go faster! I guess we both won. Let's try again because I know my number eleven can win."

PRE-READING *Compound Words*

Objective: to speculate on the origin of several words while adding to the child's vocabulary.
Materials needed: paper and crayons.

Bring to mind various compound words and talk about what they mean. Let your child illustrate the words on paper. Some examples are: sidewalk, necktie, bedroom, butterfly, cowboy, hairbrush, doorknob, and window shade. Think of others and speculate about their origin.

WEEK THREE

CHARACTER *Christmas Story*

Objective: to point to the ultimate gift by the Ultimate Giver.
Materials needed: scissors, crayons, cardboard, glue, and the activity sheet (p. 169).

Review Luke chapter 2 and the story of the Savior's birth. Relate the narrative to your child in your own words. Talk about why it would be hard for God the Father to send His only Son. Was that a very good gift for us? Illustrate the story by working on a crèche together. Glue the activity sheet to a piece of light cardboard so that the figures can stand independently. Color and cut them out. Arrange to form your very own nativity scene.

OUR WORLD *Making Rain*

Objective: to observe a natural phenomena in the weather forum.
Materials needed: a pot with a lid and water.

Boil water in a pot. Let it simmer for a while, with the lid on, until quite a bit of moisture has collected. Being careful not to scorch anybody with the steam, raise the lid and observe all the water that flows down from it. Where did it come from? How did it

get onto the lid? Use this as an illustration of the way sea water evaporates with the heat of the sun until it hits the cold of the air and forms first clouds, then rain.

WORD CONCEPTS *Volleyball*

Objective: to strike a contrast between *heavy* and *light*.
Materials needed: a good-sized rock and a balloon.

Compare the properties of the rock and the balloon. Are there any similarities? What are the differences? What can they be used for? Does one weigh more than another? Play a quick game of balloon volleyball over the backs of a few chairs, stationed in a row. Allow each player three hits on a side and state no boundaries. The player in possession of the balloon must hit it over the chairs to the other side before it touches the ground on his own side. Could this game be played with a rock?

PRE-MATH *Paper Chains*

Objective: to make something decorative that is also very countable.
Materials needed: construction paper, tape, and scissors.

Cut the paper into small strips. Loop them one inside another until a chain has been formed. Count each loop as you add them one at a time and also at the completion of the project to recheck your figures. Perhaps the chain can be hung from your Christmas tree.

PRE-READING *Place Cards*

Objective: to practice writing skills in the lettering of names.
Materials needed: index cards and markers.

Fold the cards in half. Write the name of each person who will be seated at the table for dinner on another piece of paper to be used as a reference. Your child can copy the names onto the cards. Or you might outline the letters lightly in pencil on the cards themselves for your child to trace. Think of a different seasonal emblem to be drawn on each card to make it more decorative.

WEEK FOUR

CHARACTER *Kids of the Kingdom*

Objective: to remind the child that giving should occur at all times of year and to make him aware of the needs that are all around him.

Materials needed: paper towel or toilet paper rolls, yarn, glitter, glue, paints, and a brush.

Tell the following story. Encourage your child to think of someone to encourage with a homemade gift. Make napkin rings to give to the person of his choice by cutting the paper rolls into one inch widths. Decorate as desired. Allow to dry. Wrap and deliver with lots of love.

Once upon a time, there were three good friends, Timothy, Michael, and Ashley. This had been a wonderful Christmas because each of them had found a special way to give to others.

Tim and his family opened their home on Christmas Day to a family of five children whose father had hurt his leg. Since the father could not work, the family had become very poor. But Tim and his family made sure they had lots of food and presents even if they had no money of their own.

Mike made some beautiful little gifts to take to a home where old people lived. He had a great time passing them out to each person. He talked with them and told them his favorite jokes. Even the ones who couldn't get out of bed laughed with him.

Ashley saved all the money she could earn to send to one of the missionaries in the church. It was to go toward a tape recorder

that could help the missionaries tell many people about Jesus in their very own language. Ashley hoped the tape recorder arrived just in time for Christmas.

"It's too bad Christmas is all over," Ashley sighed to the boys. "Now we won't be able to help any more people or give anything else away."

"I have an idea!" Timothy almost shouted. "Why don't we start a secret club that does special things for other people all year long? We won't tell anyone else about it, but we'll think of ideas and carry them out."

"Sure," Michael cut in. "We could fix up some of the toys we've outgrown for kids who don't have very many. We could bake cookies for our neighbors and leave them at their door. We could make cards for the older people in our church to say that they are loved . . . all kinds of things!"

"Yeah," Tim was really excited now. "We'll do lots of good deeds and keep it as our secret. We'll be a special club. We'll call ourselves 'the Kids of the Kingdom.' "

"When can we begin?" asked Ashley. "How about on the first day of the new year? Let's decide what project we want to start on."

OUR WORLD *Pinwheel*

Objective: to talk about another weather condition and its useful purpose.

Materials needed: a pencil, a push pin, paper, scissors, and the activity sheet (p. 171).

Follow the instructions on the sheet. Demonstrate how moving air can turn a wheel. Could the energy of the wind be harnessed (in certain areas of the country with the right conditions) to provide electricity for the people who live there? Are there certain times of the year when the wind is more prevalent in the place where you live?

WORD CONCEPTS *The Mixed-Up Dog*

Objective: to illustrate each of the study words for the month through word and deed.

Tell the following short story. As you narrate, let your child act out the part of the dog. When the dog is *hot*, your child can pant. When the dog is *cold*, your child can shiver. When the dog goes *out*, your child can exit the room through a doorway. When the dog comes *in*, your child can enter the room. When the dog has a full coat, your child can lumber under the *heavy* fur. When the dog gets groomed, your child can prance as *light* as can be.

There once was a dog. A furry dog. A very furry dog. He had so much hair that he could hardly walk. Whenever he ate, the hair would hang in his food. Whenever he tried to look around, the fur got in his eyes. No one could pick him up because all his fur made him so very *heavy*.

The heavy coat made him very uncomfortable as well. Whenever he was *in*, he would get so hot, he wanted out. But whenever he was *out*, the weather was so cold, he wanted in. What was to be done with this very furry dog who was always too *hot* or too *cold* and either wanted to be *in* or *out?*

There was one little boy who knew just what to do. "This dog needs to get a haircut," he said. So he took that dog, heavy with fur, to a groomer. The groomer took a pair of scissors and with a snip, snip, snip, cut off a lot of hair.

"Just right," said the boy. And he took the dog, *light* as a feather, back to his home. Now the dog was not too *hot* or too *cold*. He was just right. When he was *in*, he was happy to be in. When he was *out*, he was happy to be out. Best of all, he was no longer too *heavy* to hold; so he could snuggle right up to the little boy who had known just what he needed.

PRE-MATH   *Word Problems*

Objective: to prove the relevance of mathematical skill and to prompt your child to reason.

Materials needed: objects to help visualize the problems (pebbles, blocks, etc.).

Talk through three hypothetical word problems.

(1) Suppose your mother baked ten cookies and set them out to cool. All of a sudden, a martian landed in your kitchen and ate seven of them. How many would be left for your dessert after dinner?

(2) Pretend that it was your birthday. You invited six children to your party, but only three of them showed up. Each of them brought a present. How many more presents might you have received had everyone you invited come?

(3) Suppose you were racing some toy cars down a dirt hill. Two of them got stuck, but three of them made it the whole way. How many cars did you start the race with?

(4) Imagine you had four pennies to put in the offering at church, but in the parking lot you dropped one. How much could you give to God?

Don't become frustrated with this activity. It will stretch your child's ability to concentrate, but conceptualizing will not come easy for any preschooler. Work with each problem a little while, then move on.

PRE-READING   *Lettered Objects*

Objective: to recognize an alphabetical letter and find at least one object whose name begins with that letter.

Materials needed: paper, markers, and tape.

Draw several letters on individual sheets of paper. Stick a piece of tape onto the backs of the papers in such a way that they will stick to the objects that they are placed upon. Hand a sheet to your child and encourage him to find something around the house that begins with the same letter. Show him how to tape the letter onto the object as an identification. Do the same with each of the letters you have chosen.

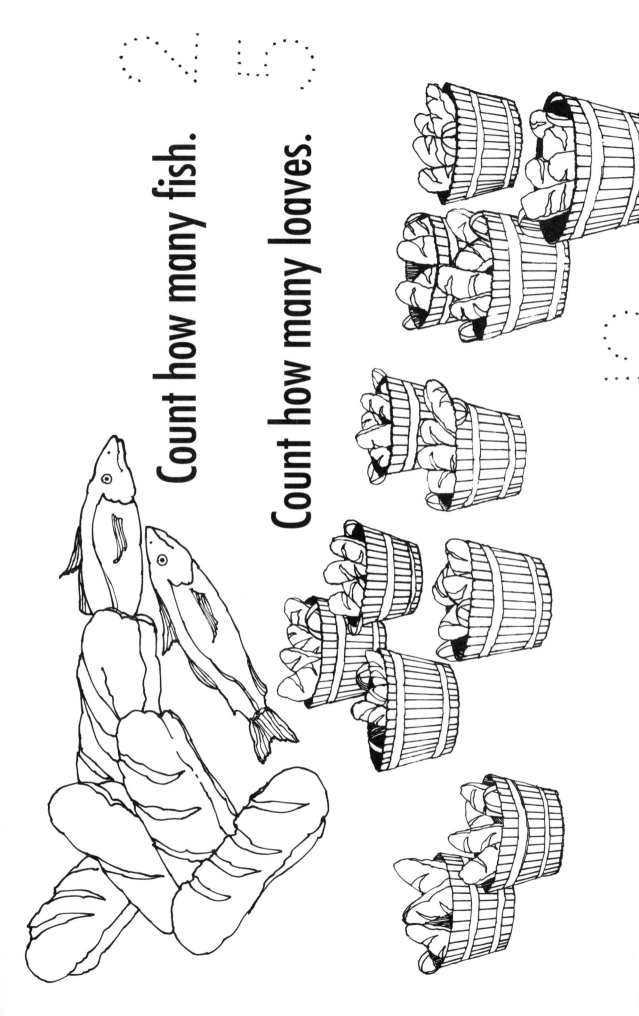

Count how many fish.

Count how many loaves.

Count how many baskets left over.

December 1

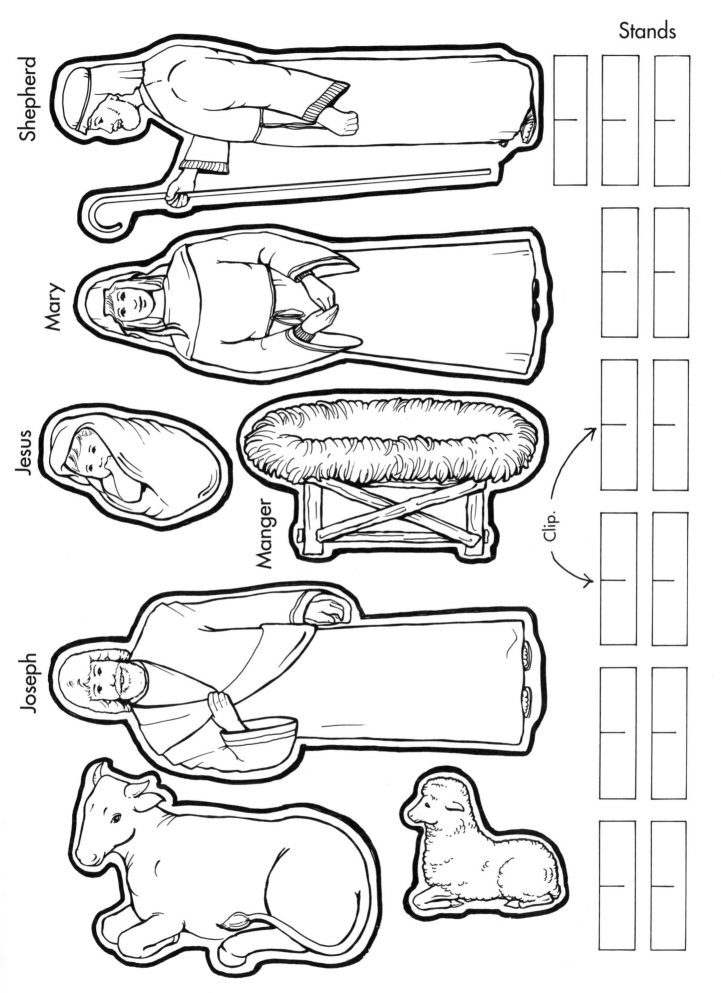

Stands

Shepherd

Mary

Jesus

Manger

Clip.

Joseph

December 2

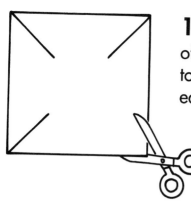

1. Take a square piece of paper and cut a slit toward the center from each corner.

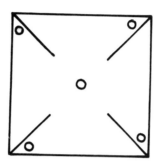

2. Cut or punch a hole in the center and also to the right of each cut.

3. Fold the corner holes to align with the center hole.

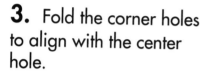

4. Slide the push pin through the holes and into the eraser end of the pencil.

5. Blow gently on the pinwheel to see the results of the wind.

INDEX